Ah...That's

Gas

First published 2021 by The O'Brien Press Ltd.
12 Terenure Road East, Rathgar, Dublin 6, D06 HD27, Ireland.
Tel: +353 1 4923333 Fax: +353 1 4922777

Email: books@obrien.ie. Website: www.obrien.ie
The O'Brien Press is a member of Publishing Ireland.

ISBN 978-1-78849-295-9

1 3 5 7 9 10 8 6 4 2
21 23 25 24 22

Printed by L&C Printing Group, Poland.

The paper in this book is produced using pulp from managed forests.

Published in

DUBLIN

UNESCO
City of Literature

Ah... That's Gas

The ads, fads & mad happenings that swept the Irish nation

Sarah Cassidy and Kunak McGann

THE O'BRIEN PRESS
DUBLIN

A

Adam's Virtual Hug

Six-year-old space fanatic Adam King captured the hearts of a locked-down nation when he appeared on the 2020 *Late Late Toy Show* and introduced everyone to his virtual hug. The response was extraordinary, with Adam 'e-meeting' astronaut Commander Chris Hadfield and receiving congratulatory letters from the Taoiseach and even US President Biden himself. Adam's virtual hug cards sold out everywhere, and there were hearts lit up on buildings across the country. Never before had a socially distanced and affection-starved Ireland needed one of Adam's hugs more.

Aer Arann

In 1970, this regional airline's maiden flight took place from Galway to the Aran Islands. The first flights were about eighteen minutes long on a twin-engine, ten-seater plane to a landing strip on Inis Mór, and would set you back the princely sum of five Irish pounds. No duty free though.

'Ah … That's Bass!'

The slogan for the British ale used in the classic 1978 ad

featuring the Dubliners, with Ronnie Drew delivering the punchline. Young children loved the line and often mimicked it when getting stuck into their beakers of milk. To this day, there are forty- and fifty-somethings who have to follow every sup of a pint with 'Ah ... that's Bass!'

Ah, Ref!

The 1998 All-Ireland hurling semi-final between Clare and Offaly took some winning. After a 1–13 draw, the replay caused all sorts of controversy when the ref mistakenly ended the game several minutes earlier than he should have, giving Clare the victory. Incensed Offaly fans staged a sit-down protest on the pitch in Croker. The game was replayed (again) a week later in Semple Stadium, with the midlands county emerging as the eventual winners. Took them an Offaly long time to get there, though ...

Angela's Ashes

Irish American Frank McCourt's 1996 memoir about his family's impoverished life in Limerick was a huge hit all around the world and went on to win a Pulitzer. The book was such a success that it spawned an entire subgenre, the 'misery memoir', and, God bless us, few nationalities do that better than the Irish. You have to give us that.

Angel Delight

The 1970s was the era of tinned fruit cocktail and sugar sandwiches, so when Angel Delight came along it brought a touch of class to midweek desserts. A powder whisked with milk and set in the fridge to form a light mousse, it came in classic flavours like strawberry, banana, butterscotch and chocolate. Some of the more ambitious but less popular flavours were tea, popcorn and bubblegum. Nothing angelic about those.

Annalise Murphy

Despite being an island nation, Ireland has never really held its own when it comes to sailing, so we were overjoyed in 2013 when 23-year-old Dubliner Annalise Murphy bagged a gold medal at the European Sailing Championships in the women's laser radial category. She had already made a bit of a splash at the 2012 Olympics in London and went on to score a silver medal in Rio in 2016. Murphy celebrated her European gold medal with a 99 ice cream cone from the iconic Teddy's in Dun Laoghaire. You can take the girl out of Dublin …

Anything Goes

Keen to tap into the youth audience, RTÉ launched its first Saturday-morning children's programme in 1980, and it ran for six years. Fronted by Aonghus McAnally, Mary Fitzgerald, Kathy Parke and Dave Heffernan, it was a mix of chat, make and do, pop videos and interviews with the likes of U2 and Thin Lizzy, with a studio full of adorably unpredictable children. The end credits signalled the beginning of wall-to-wall sports coverage – and parents yelling at their kids to stop wasting the day and go out and get some fresh air.

'Aon Focal Eile'

Doing for dungarees what Elvis did for white-sequinned jumpsuits, Richie Kavanagh exploded onto the Irish music scene in 1996 with this cheeky little number that gave kids permission to repeatedly say the word 'focal' (pronounced 'fuckle'). An impassioned song about the difficulty of learning our native language, to this day 'Aon Focal Eile' is still the only Irish that a lot of people know.

Aussie Soaps

In the 1980s Ireland was obsessed with Aussie soaps.

First it was *Neighbours*, required lunchtime viewing for schoolkids. We couldn't get enough of Scott and Charlene and the goings-on on Ramsay Street. Then RTÉ was the first broadcaster outside of Oz to air *Home and Away*, and we dreamed of surfing on Summer Bay with Shane and Angel, being adopted by Pippa or growled at by Alf 'Flamin' Galah' Stewart.

B

B*Witched

This Irish-dancing foursome hit the charts in the late 1990s and had teenagers doing their 1, 2, 3s up and down the nation's dance floors. The double-denimed songstresses released two albums and eight singles, with their first four singles all hitting the UK No 1 spot. And they fought like their Da as well.

Bachelors Walk

An RTÉ comedy-drama broadcast in the early 2000s, *Bachelors Walk* centred around the lives of three men: film critic Raymond (Don Wycherley), barrister Michael (Simon Delaney) and all-round chancer Barry (Keith McErlean), who shared a house on the famous Dublin street. Viewers, revelling in the home-grown content, spent their time pointing out 'I know that place', 'I was there last Friday' and 'There's no way he'd end up in that street on his way home from Mulligan's'.

Back to the Future

One of the biggest box-office smashes of 1985, *Back to the Future* featured Doc Brown's time machine: the iconic silver DeLorean with its distinctive gull-wing doors.

These highly collectible cars were manufactured in Belfast for a few short years in the early 1980s. Michael J. Fox starred as Marty McFly in his trademark orange body warmer, who, thanks to the time machine, befriended his dad and made out with his mom. Great Scott!

Balcony Bingo

Covid restrictions may have meant an end to in-person socialising and most forms of entertainment, but Michael Larkin, a resident of a block of flats in Ringsend, had the genius idea to start Balcony Bingo: a socially distant version of the classic numbers game. Bingo fanatics will tell you that it has always been about community and not gambling; the success of balcony bingo attests to this. Winning is just the jackpot in the full house. Lucky for some!

Ballykissangel

Running from 1996 to 2001, *Ballykissangel* was perfect Sunday-evening viewing, with a range of gas characters getting themselves into scrapes in a sleepy Irish village. Taking a leaf out of *The Thorn Birds'* book, it featured a long-running 'will they/won't they' romance between Father Peter and pub landlady Assumpta. Plot spoiler: they did. Kind of.

The Ballymaloe Cookbook

Before the relish, there was the cookbook. Published in 1977 and focusing on locally sourced ingredients, the iconic book by Myrtle Allen could be found in every self-respecting Irish household. Myrtle passed the torch to daughter-in-law Darina Allen, who has continued her legacy alongside her own daughter-in-law, Rachel Allen. Between them they've taught half of Ireland how to cook.

Ballyragget Win

When St Patrick's Ballyragget from Kilkenny won the Leinster Intermediate Club Hurling final in 2017, it's fair to say that celebrations got a little bit out of hand. The national press gleefully published photographs taken at a private party with one lad posing, scantily clad, with the cup and not one but two equally scantily clad strippers. The coverage brought significant attention to the club, with unconfirmed reports of a spike in transfer requests.

Banshee Bones

You can keep your Wheelies and your Chickatees, your Hot Lips and your Meanies; when it came to the best savoury snack for your ten pence, Banshee Bones stole the show. There was widespread disappointment when they were discontinued, and unrestrained joy when Tayto announced their return for Halloween 2020. Laden with salt and vinegar flavouring, for true addicts just reading this paragraph will be enough to kick your salivary glands into overdrive.

Barefoot Hurling

There has been no sporting performance quite like that of Michael 'Babs' Keating in the 1971 All-Ireland hurling final. With Tipp playing against the old enemy, Kilkenny, the pressure was on. But a cobbler's nail came through one of Babs' freshly repaired boots, and once he threw that boot off, he was lopsided and had no choice but to discard the other. And sure then, without boots to keep them on, his socks slid off too. This didn't stop him from hitting seven points over the bar to help his team to victory. Barefoot brilliance.

The Beast from the East

On 22 February 2018, Anticyclone Hartmut, originating from an Arctic outbreak, hit Ireland, bringing with it unusually low temperatures and extremely heavy snowfall. Nicknamed the Beast from the East, the storm was so bad that many roads were inaccessible and schools and businesses across the country were forced to close. To make matters worse, wily shoppers stockpiled loaves of bread in anticipation of being snowed in, causing widespread shortages. Where to get a fresh sliced pan was the topic on everyone's lips.

The Beatbox

The Beatbox was a revolutionary simulcast – music videos broadcast simultaneously on RTÉ telly and radio from 11.30am to 1.30pm on a Sunday. Running from the late 1980s until 1995, it featured a range of presenters: Barry Lang, Simon Young, Peter Collins and Ian Dempsey. Viewers could call in to log their vote in the Battle of the Bands or send in actual postcards to win the lyrics quiz (with awesome prizes like all-too-cool ghetto blasters). The only dilemma was the timing: you had to dodge mass not to miss the start and get yer ma to put off the Sunday dinner till after 1.30pm (sure the roast beef would be ruined).

Bertie Ahern

Love him or hate him, surely the most bizarre appearance by Bertie Ahern must be when he turned up in a 2010 ad for the Irish *News of the World*. After a political career spanning over thirty years, he was offered a sports column (sure, why wouldn't he be?), and his turn in the ad saw him squished into a lad's cupboard, with a cup of tea and gingernut biscuits. Jaysus.

Big Snow of '82

The winter that went down in Irish legend as the worst in living memory, when the whole country ground to a halt and Irish children finally got to make some decent snowmen. With widespread electricity cuts, 100,000 homes and businesses lost power. There were actual bread riots, and the government had to requisition 50,000 gallons of milk to combat the dairy drought in the capital. We thought it was the worst we'd see. And then came the Beast from the East ...

Blackboard Jungle

This quiz show for secondary-school teams, hosted by Ray D'Arcy, first aired in 1991. Seven series, six categories, five rounds of questions, up to three times weekly, broadcast on Network 2. The funky set had teams sitting behind giant pencils, with a backdrop of textbook pages. The prizes were everything from *Blackboard Jungle* hoodies to thesauruses, personal stereos, camcorders and even a minibus for your school. Nerdy heaven.

Bond, James Bond

With Ireland's reputation for witty, suave and good-looking men, it was only a matter of time before one of them was chosen to be James Bond. Navan man Pierce Brosnan took the distinction, playing Bond in four movies between 1995 and 2002. During that time, he saved the British economy, averted war between Britain and China, disarmed a nuclear bomb, and stopped North Korea invading South Korea – all while delivering some really top-class punny lines and being shaken, not stirred. You wouldn't be able.

The Boomtown Rats

The Rats were the first Irish band to have a UK No 1, with 1978's 'Rat Trap', following it up with the global smash 'I Don't Like Mondays'. By 1980, they were at the height of their fame and due to play a homecoming gig to 7,500 fans at Leopardstown Racecourse. When the courts refused to grant permission for the gig to go ahead, another venue had to be found. The band eventually played to 10,000 fans at Leixlip Castle on 2 March. And the crowd went wild!

Boot-Cut Jeans

According to the presenters of *Head to Toe*, this classic jean, which comes out in a slight flare from the knee, was the most flattering of cuts – balancing out the hips, apparently. Good job, too, as for some reason tops in the '90s were always an inch too short and stopped somewhere around the belly button. Alarming rumours abound that the boot-cut is now making a comeback ...

Bosco

This much-loved red-haired, living-in-a-box puppet entertained Irish kids through 386 episodes, with production finally ending in 1987. Regular segments on the show included animations Gregory Gráinneog, the Tongue Twister Twins, The McSpuds and Faherty's Garden, and exciting visits to the Zoo or the Cadbury's factory through the Magic Door. 'Knock, knock, open wide, and see what's on the other side ...' And there was no containing the excitement on the very rare occasions that Bosco let the viewers see inside his box.

Boxing Olympic Medals

Ireland's first Olympic gold medal for boxing came in 1992 in Barcelona, with Dublin southpaw Michael Carruth securing victory in the welterweight division. Meanwhile, his Antrim teammate, Wayne McCullough, was fighting his way to a bantamweight silver. A hero's welcome awaited the pair, who inspired many young men and women to follow in their footsteps.

Boyzone on TV

It was just another Friday night in 1993, but life for the nation's teenage girls would never be the same again. A group of Dublin lads danced their way onto our screens on *The Late Late Show* – no singing, no instruments, just fellas in varying states of undress busting moves while Gay and the audience watched on in bewilderment. Despite this dubious introduction to the world, Boyzone went on to become one of the biggest boy bands in the world, selling 25 million records worldwide. Life really is a rollercoaster ...

Brady's Celebration

Going into the match against Italy during the 2016 Euros in France, Ireland had only managed one point in the championship. But then Robbie Brady turned everything around with a goal in the eighty-fifth minute, smashing us into the knockout stages. When an emotional Brady ran over to the sidelines to hug his girlfriend and brother, they were crying, we were crying, you were crying!

'Breakfast Time Back Home'

Picture it: Sean wakes up in the middle of the night, sirens wailing in the New York streets. He pops to his local corner store for the makings of a Galtee fry-up. The girlfriend is roused by the sizzle of his sausages. 'Sean? It's three o'clock in the morning!' 'Yeah, but it's breakfast time back home.' This 1994 ad hits you right in the diaspora.

Brexit

Most. Discussed. Subject. Ever.

Brooklyn

Based on the novel by Colm Tóibín, this 2015 movie
starred Saoirse Ronan and Domhnall Gleeson. Set
in 1951, it's the story of Eilis Lacey, who grows up in
Enniscorthy and emigrates to – you've guessed it –
New York, where she meets a charming young Italian
American, Tony Fiorello. Her return home later in the
novel sets up a love triangle with local bachelor Jim
Farrell, with the audience torn on which man Eilis should
choose. #TeamTony #TeamJim

Brown Sauce

This condiment has its fair share of fans here, but its
controversial appearance in the 2003 movie *Intermission*
did wonders for its 'love it or hate it' reputation.
Characters played by Cillian Murphy and Colin Farrell
sink mugs of tea laced with the stuff, with Colin
declaring, 'That's f*ckin' delish, man.' Don't knock it till
you've tried it.

Bus Lane

The country's first official bus lane came into operation
in 1980. Just 250 metres long, the contraflow lane ran up

Parliament Street and was designed to alleviate delays for bus commuters from areas like Tallaght, Crumlin and Ballyfermot. From small beginnings ...

C

Callcards

First introduced by Telecom Éireann in 1988, Ireland's phone cards could be used in payphones and came in denominations from 5 to 100 units, for £2–£16. There were 324 different designs issued between 1988 and 2006, featuring everything from the Rock of Cashel to Irish legends, Disney movies to Garth Brooks. Always handy to have one in the wallet when you needed collecting from the bus.

Calor Housewife of the Year

This popular competition first went live on TV in 1982, with Gay Byrne as host, and ran until 1995. Like a Rose of Tralee for the more mature woman, hopeful participants went head-to-head on their cookery, nurturing and basic household management skills, with a gas cooker as the top prize. The competition was eventually abandoned amid complaints that too many finalists were working outside the home. The cheek.

Cartoon Saloon

This Kilkenny-based studio first came to world attention when their hand-drawn animated feature film, *The Secret of Kells* (2010) was nominated for an Oscar. Since then, they've notched up another four nominations – and that elusive win can only be around the corner. In the meantime, they always give us an excuse to put on our glad rags and wait up till the wee hours for the results. Pass the popcorn!

Cascarino's Passport

Tony Cascarino made eighty-eight appearances for the Ireland team, including at the 1988 Euros and the 1990 and 1994 World Cup Finals, qualifying via his Irish maternal grandfather from Westport. Thing is, his grandfather wasn't a blood relative after all, making Tony ineligible to ever have played for Ireland. He went public with the explosive story in his 2000 autobiography, but the official position was very much one of letting bygones be bygones. Sure, didn't he give us our money's worth anyway? Fair play to the lad.

CB Radios

A forerunner of social media, CB radios were mad popular for a long stretch in the 1970s and early '80s, with the release of movies like *Smokey and the Bandit* and *Convoy* (starring hunky heart-throbs Burt Reynolds and Kris Kristofferson, respectively). In real life, there was something wonderfully nerdy about folks in Sligo and Westmeath spending Saturday nights in their bedrooms using phrases like 'Breaker one-nine', 'Smokey Bear' and 'Ten four, good buddy'. Undecipherable to the uninitiated.

Celtic Tiger

Ireland of the Celtic Tiger is almost unrecognisable now. Back then, weekend trips to NYC to stock up on your Tommy 'Highflier' and your Ralph 'La'wren' were common, as were holiday homes in Bulgaria, and more credit-card debt than you could shake a platinum-ringed finger at. For some, the Celtic Tiger roared, while for others it merely miaowed quietly in the corner.

Champagne Supernova

Raheny man Dave Grennan has been searching the skies with his home-built telescope for years. He has been rewarded by finding not one but three supernovae (exploding stars) since 2010, the latest of which was 170 million years old, a hundred times bigger than our own sun, and 170 quadrillion miles away. On his discovery, far from reaching for the champers, Dave and his wife

instead settled for a 'nice strong cup of tea'. Looking at
the stars but feet firmly on the ground, that fella.

Cheltenham

Cheltenham 2020? Don't even start. When it comes to
splitting the country, it's the new Saipan.

Cidona

If it was the 1980s and a special occasion that called for a
bottle of wine, there was bound to be a bottle of Cidona
there for the kids. A sparkling apple-based soft drink
with only a passing relationship to its alcoholic cousin,
it still somehow gave young 'uns an air of sophistication.
Not just your ordinary mineral.

Circle of Friends

Based on the Maeve Binchy novel, this film follows the
trials and romantic tribulations of a trio of friends at
university in Dublin in the 1950s. One of the girls, Benny
(Minnie Driver, funny, loveable, slightly dodgy Irish
accent), falls for medical student Jack (Chris O'Donnell,
handsome, rich, very dodgy Irish accent), though alas the
path of true love doesn't run smooth. But with a closing

line of 'Bless me, father, for I have sinned', we can only assume that Benny and Jack both got their happy ending.

Clapping on the Doorsteps

In the first lockdown of 2020, with everyone feeling stressed and under siege from the pandemic, our options for showing appreciation for our frontline worker family, friends and neighbours were limited. In late March, gratitude spilled out open windows and over onto the doorsteps as we all came together to clap and cheer. A much-needed feel-good moment.

Commander Chris Hadfield

Canadian astronaut Chris Hadfield is the ultimate honorary Irishman. In 2013, he duetted with The Chieftains – they were in Houston, Texas; he was at the International Space Station. A few days later he transmitted the first Irish-language message from space with his tweet 'Tá Éire fíorálainn! Land of green hills and dark beer. With capital Dublin glowing in the Irish night.' And in 2014, he became an ambassador for Irish tourism, even trying out the obligatory bit of balancing a sliotar on a hurley. No question about it, he's one of us.

The Commitments

Based on the book by Roddy Doyle, *The Commitments* film was released in 1991, and it sent the whole country into a tizzy looking for its soul. The story of the world's hardest-working band, the combination of a talented young cast, whip-smart dialogue and cracking soul tunes ensured that their cover of 'Mustang Sally' appeared on radio playlists for years to come. The best Irish band ever? Sure, U2 were sh*ttin' themselves.

Concorde

The Air France Concorde caused a bit of a stir when it first touched down at Dublin Airport in 1983. The supersonic aircraft was there to pick up passengers, including VIPs like the French Ambassador to Ireland and the Lord Mayor of Dublin, for the Prix de l'Arc de Triomphe horse race in Paris. Ordinary punters forked out no less than £483 for the privilege, including flight, hotel and tickets. Champers on board too, of course. Nothing like necking a bit of bubbly while you break the sound barrier.

Contraceptive Train

Back in the 1970s, Irish women were legally prevented from being prescribed the contraceptive pill, unlike their sisters in Northern Ireland. In May 1971, a group from the Irish Women's Liberation Movement met at Connolly Station in Dublin, boarding the Belfast train on a mission to purchase the pill when they got there. Of course, the pill wasn't available in Belfast without prescription, so the women instead bought condoms and other contraceptives, as well as hundreds of packets of aspirin, knowing that Customs officials wouldn't know what the pill looked like anyway!

Cork Six-in-a-Row

Dominating the sport through the 2000s and 2010s, Cork became footballing record breakers in 2016 when they claimed a sixth consecutive All-Ireland Ladies' Senior Football title. The 2016 final was a close call, with only a point between them and their rivals, Dublin. Cork also won an unbelievable eleven consecutive League titles in the same period. Up the Rebels!

The Corrs

When this Dundalk band arrived on the scene in 1995 with their single 'Runaway', much was made of how easy on the eye sisters Sharon, Caroline and Andrea – and even brother Jim – were. Their music blended pop with traditional airs and instruments, including the bodhrán, fiddle and tin whistle, and for a world still captivated by Riverdance and all things Irish, the combination proved seductive. The band sold over forty-five million records worldwide before taking time apart to pursue solo careers and raise families. And Jim has been known to come out with the odd controversial comment. Ahem.

Cricket

Ireland is not traditionally a cricket-loving country, but our performance at the 2007 World Cup made everyone sit up and take notice. Our national team, made up of teachers, postmen and farmers, managed to clinch victory over cricket giants Pakistan, knocking them out of the tournament in what was a colossal upset. The win elevated Ireland to tenth in the world and had us all reaching for the rules of cricket to find out exactly what it was we were suddenly good at.

Crystal Swing

This Cork country music trio had a viral hit in 2010 with 'He Drinks Tequila', racking up over a million views on YouTube and appearing on Irish and US TV. Mary Murray-Burke and her then-teenagers, son Derek and daughter Dervla, had a lovely, wholesome showband way about them, which contrasted wonderfully with the young brother and sister duetting about yer man drinking hard liquor while yer wan peeled off her stockings and talked dirty in Spanish. *Dios mío*!

D

Dana

The original Derry Girl, Dana won the 1970 Eurovision
Song Contest, perched on a stool in a white mini-dress
singing 'All Kinds of Everything' at just eighteen years
of age. The song sold two million copies worldwide
and launched her illustrious music career. Decades
later, in 1997 and at the tender age of 46, Dana began
her political career with an unsuccessful bid at the
Irish Presidency but was later elected as MEP for
Connacht–Ulster, serving from 1999 to 2004. All kinds
of everything, indeed.

Dancing Guinness Man

One of the most popular Irish ads of all time, this 1994
offering starred Joe McKinney throwing shapes and
wiggling eyebrows while he waits for the barman to pour
his pint. The distinctive music featured, a mambo called
'Guaglione' by Perez Prado, hit the No 1 spot and was
often heard on the radio and in pubs and nightclubs,
where people threw lots of their own shapes to it. Here,
hold my pint!

Darndale Stowaways

In 1985, two Dublin lads – Keith Byrne and Noel Murray, aged ten and thirteen – decided to head to America to try and meet *The A-Team*'s B.A. Baracus. Sure, why not? They hopped on the DART, sneaked on to a ferry to Holyhead, boarded a train to London, then Heathrow Airport, and managed to blag their way on to a flight to New York. They finally came a cropper when they asked a New York cop for 'the way into town'. They were put up in a five-star hotel in the care of no fewer than five security guards before being returned home safely. Little legends.

Derry Girls

From the moment *Derry Girls* hit our screens in 2018, the rave reviews were in: this 1990s-set sitcom was original, authentic and, above all, absolutely hilarious. The series follows Erin, Clare, Orla, Michelle and English Boy-turned-Derry-Girl James as they navigate secondary school amidst the turmoil of the Troubles. Some of the more memorable scenes include teenagers listing the differences between Catholics and Protestants, the gang clogging up a toilet with hash scones during a wake, and Erin's family trying to decide how many bags of chipper chips to order.

The Diceman

Anyone who regularly walked down Grafton Street in the 1980s will remember the Diceman. Scottish-born Thom McGinty was an actor and street performer, named for a shop that he advertised and best known for staying completely still while wearing the most flamboyant costumes and body paint – only moving to give a pantomime wink to the delighted punters who darted in to drop money at his feet. He became such a Dublin icon that, after his untimely death in 1995, his coffin was carried the length of Grafton Street, bringing it to a standstill. A fitting tribute.

Diving Hero

In June 2018, the world was captivated by the story of the Thai boys' soccer team caught in a flooded underground cave. When Co. Clare man Jim Warny heard the news, he picked up the phone and offered his cave-diving skills to the rescue effort. Within forty-eight hours he was on a plane to Bangkok, and he was the diver that carried the team's coach to safety on the third and final day of the rescue. What an absolute ledge.

'Don't Forget Your Shovel'

Released in 1985, this was Lilywhite Christy Moore's first solo single after leaving the band Moving Hearts, and it spent seven weeks at No 1. Written by Christie Hennessy, it was a humorous take on the experience of the Irish on building sites in the UK, and the video followed Christy and his mates as they toil away, wearing nothing but jeans and sandals. Builder's tan, ahoy!

'Do You Want Your Old Lobby Washed Down?'

Thought to originate in Co. Cork, this traditional folk song offers up a bit of manual labour in return for a few bob. Made popular in 1979 by folk legend Brendan Shine, nimbly playing away on his accordion, there are many who take the song at face value – but there's no way that's not a *double entendre*. Ooh-er missus.

dublinbikes

Launched in 2009, this ambitious bike-rental scheme was similar to that already operating in sixteen countries across the world. Starting with 450 bikes across forty hire stations, it quickly grew to 1,600 bikes and 116 stations.

Over twenty-eight million journeys later, it could be described as a wheelie successful initiative ...

Dublin City Women's Invasionary Force

Dublin's Forty Foot is a great spot for swimmers to brave the cold waters of the Irish Sea all year round. Traditionally for men only, it wasn't until 1974 that women asserted their right to swim there too. The Dublin City Women's Invasionary Force showed up in July of that year, swimsuits on and placards held aloft. They were angrily told that 'there was a time when no self-respecting women would be in here'. Undeterred, self-respecting women have been swimming there ever since.

Dublin Marathon

The first Dublin Marathon was held on the October bank holiday in 1980, starting and finishing on St Stephen's Green. In all, 2,000 people paid the £1.50 to register, and 1,421 of them finished the race. The women's winner was Carey May, and the men's was Dick Hooper, who went on to win twice more. Back in those low-tech days, everything was done by hand – the race programme, numbers and results – and the distance was measured off a car speedometer. It may have been 'a wee bit short'.

Dublin Millennium

Dublin celebrated its thousandth birthday in 1988 with a year of celebrations. In the depths of a recession, this was a welcome opportunity for the county to let loose and kick up its heels, including a millennium parade, new sculptures of Molly Malone and Anna Livia, and a giant seventy-foot Gulliver floating down the River Liffey. And there was plenty of merchandise too: the new fifty-pence coins, the badges, the tie pins, the milk bottles, the decanters, the vases, the jewellery. The collectors were only beside themselves.

The Dubs' Six-in-a-Row

In the strangest of years for GAA, in December 2020, the Dubs clinched their record sixth All-Ireland football win in a row. They bagged their first goal just thirteen seconds after throw-in, and though Mayo fought back hard, in the end the writing was on the wall. With no fans at the game, Hill 16 was eerily silent, but you can bet their supporters were cheering and screaming at the telly back home, having kept the Sam Maguire in the capital for another year.

Dunnes Protestors

In July 1984, Dunnes Stores workers Mary Manning and Karen Gearon were suspended for refusing to handle grapefruit imported from South Africa, in protest at that country's horrific apartheid policies. Ten of their co-workers went on strike in solidarity and remained that way – on just £21 a week strike pay – for almost three years, until April 1987 when the Irish government finally banned the import of South African produce. Nelson Mandela met and publicly thanked the inspirational strikers when he visited Dublin in 1990.

E

Eamonn Coghlan

The year 1983 was a good one for 'the Chairman of the Boards': the thirty-year-old Drimnagh man broke his own record for the indoor mile and then went on to take the 5,000m gold at the World Athletics Championships in Helsinki. Anyone who watched that race will remember the last lap, from when Coghlan made his move to take the lead, comfortably romping home in the last stretch. His win went down in Irish sporting history and lifted the spirits of the nation. Lump-in-the-throat viewing.

Eat the Peach

Taken from a TS Eliot quote – 'Do I dare to eat a peach?' – this 1986 Irish film was inspired by the true-life story of two brothers-in-law from Granard, Co. Longford, who watched an old Elvis Presley movie about a motorcycle Wall of Death, a giant, high-walled wooden cylinder where centrifugal force keeps the motorbike rider up, circling at speed inside. The two lads were inspired to build their own Wall of Death out in the Irish countryside, and the people there had never seen the like – neither had the film audience.

EEC

After voting by an overwhelming 83% in favour, Ireland was welcomed into the loving arms of our European Economic Community partners on 1 January 1973. Joining brought access to a multimillion-consumer market, free travel, the Common Agricultural Policy and social and structural funding. As we were then very much the poor cousin of Europe, Ireland gained billions in additional funding over the next few decades. *Irlande, douze points*!

Eircodes

The Irish version of the postcode was officially introduced here in 2014. Seemingly nonsensical jumbles of letters and numbers, it's like they go out of their way not to be remembered.

Electric Picnic

The first Electric Picnic took place in 2004, with 10,000 people attending the 'boutique music festival' in Stradbally, Co. Laois one sunny September Saturday. It is now a three-day long festival that has played host to the likes of Billie Eilish, Noel Gallagher, Fatboy Slim and

Chic. Famed for its laid-back vibes, eclectic crowd and delicious food stalls, the festival is the highlight of the year for Irish music fans. Weather permitting, of course.

Electronic Voting

E-voting was first trialled in Ireland in a number of constituencies in 2002. Not ones to dip our toe in the water, the government went all gung-ho, buying 7,500 voting machines despite growing concerns about security and privacy. Eventually, they were forced into a complete U-turn and the whole debacle cost the taxpayer €55 million. But not to worry, we managed to offload the machines for a handy €70,000. Phew!

Enya

In 1988, the Donegal songstress took the world by storm with her smash-hit single 'Orinoco Flow'. She went on to become the best-selling female artist in the world, with sales of over 80 million albums. She has since taken her own advice and sailed away, sailed away, sailed away from the limelight.

Euro

On 1 January 2002, Ireland's retail officially changed over to the euro. The euro was worth nearly 79p, and the government had distributed 1.4 million euro-calculators to help people with the conversion. Despite the relatively smooth transition, the Central Bank confirms that nearly €350 million worth of old Irish punts and coins remains at large. Probably worth a dig down the back of the sofa.

Euromillionaire

The whole country was delighted for Limerick woman Dolores McNamara when she won €115 million on the Euromillions in 2005, then Europe's largest-ever lottery jackpot, catapulting her onto Ireland's rich list. Her first order of business was buying not only herself but all six of her children new homes. Irish mammies are the best, and rich Irish mammies are the bestest!

Eurovision

Ireland has won more Eurovision top spots than any other country, but four wins in five years in the 1990s was unbelievable, even for us. Linda Martin's 'Why Me?' kicked off the run of good luck in 1992, followed swiftly by Niamh Kavanagh with 'In Your Eyes', then Paul Harrington and Charlie McGettigan and their 'Rock 'n' Roll Kids', and finally Eimear Quinn's 'The Voice' in 1996. When it comes to putting together a sweet melody, a catchy chorus and – what the hell – another rousing key change, Ireland truly is a world leader.

F

Fair City

Our very first visit to Carrigstown was back in 1989, with RTÉ taking on the big hitters like *EastEnders* and *Corrie*, showing we can do our own urban drama of love triangles, freak accidents and shock twists just as well as anyone. We were all perched on the edge of our seats watching a priest's affair, half-siblings getting it on, and a crime boss killed by his own stepson. But let's face it, nothing could come close to the suspense of following Paul Brennan's tumultuous love life.

'Fairytale of New York'

A duet recorded by the Pogues and Kirsty MacColl and arguably the best Christmas song ever. The first line, 'It was Christmas Eve, babe', is enough to immediately get you in the festive spirit. And with yer man in the drunk tank singing 'The Rare Old Mountain Dew' and the NYPD lads singing 'Galway Bay', it's Irish and we're keeping it.

Far and Away

Released in 1992 and starring then husband-and-wife megastars Tom Cruise and Nicole Kidman, *Far and Away* featured some of the worst Irish accents ever committed to celluloid. Though what woman could possibly resist the Oirish charm offensive: 'Yer a corker, Shannon. What a corker you are!' I'm weak at the knees.

Fat Frog

Could this be the most iconic ad of the 1980s? An animated song featuring a frog jumping around the swamp and playing his guitar, complete with a trio of amphibian backing singers. He wasn't shy about telling us about his big, fat tummy (like no other water ice), and the fruity flavour from his toes to his eyes. A good helping of food colouring meant that you could never have one of these on the sly – your completely green tongue would always give you away.

Father Ted

Are those cows small or far away? Go on, go on, go on, go on, go on. Down with this sort of thing! Will we ever stop talking about *Father Ted*? The sitcom first aired in 1995 and is undoubtedly the most quoted TV show in Irish history. Or is it? That would be an ecumenical matter.

F-bomb

The Late Late Toy Show always brings with it a tingle of nervous excitement that one of the kids is going to say something outrageous. In 2020, little did we know that the outrage would come from the lips of host Ryan Tubridy himself. When faced with an explosive bottle of fizzy orange, Ryan inadvertently dropped an F-bomb and, moments later, locked guilty eyes with the camera. If Ryan is to be believed, it wasn't an F-bomb but a B-bomb. But a classic live TV moment either way. We'll take it!

Féile

Long before Electric Picnic there was The Trip to Tipp. During the 1990s, thousands of teenagers and twenty-somethings descended on Semple Stadium to see acts like The Stunning, Hothouse Flowers, The Cranberries and even The Prodigy live on stage. With so many unsupervised youths away from home for the first time, poor Thurles was left looking like the scene of a zombie apocalypse.

Flahavan's Tracksuit

Back in the 1980s, a snazzy white, green and red tracksuit was modelled in the Flahavan's ad by then-child actor Andrew Scott (who went on to become *Sherlock*'s Moriarty). You could snag yourself one by collecting enough tokens from packets of Flahavan's porridge, which meant eating a WHOLE LOTTA oats. But when you finally did – you were fit, cool AND regular. Result.

Floozie in the Jacuzzi

Commissioned for Dublin's millennium, the Anna Livia monument was a brass statue inspired by the character from *Finnegans Wake* by James Joyce. Installed in the centre of O'Connell Street, she was soon fondly nicknamed 'The Floozie in the Jacuzzi' (as well as other rhyming and less complimentary names). With the structure difficult to keep clean and free from rubbish, the Council decided to remove her in 2001. And of course, the Spire was later erected in a nearby spot. The irony of losing a magnificent woman and gaining a giant phallic symbol.

Floppy Disks

Young people nowadays, with their 'clouds' and their online transfers, look askance at the idea of a 3½ inch square plastic disk for conveying data. Clapping eyes on one of those good old 5¼ inch floppies would really raise an eyebrow.

Foot-and-Mouth

Ireland's first outbreak of Foot-and-Mouth since World War II happened in spring 2001. The government were taking no chances and acted swiftly, closing forest parks, football pitches and playgrounds, Dublin Zoo and Fota Wildlife Park. Gatherings like the St Patrick's Day festivities were cancelled, and we had to douse our shoes in basins of chemicals before setting foot in schools, offices and airports. Our soles had never been cleaner.

Free a Nipper!

There were few '80s children who didn't pester their parents to 'Free a nipper!' In a clever marketing campaign launched in 1985 by Maxol, Brendan Grace encouraged motorists to collect tokens for every trip to the petrol station and trade them in for what were, it has to be said, fairly pathetic-looking furry hand puppets. The country fell for it hook, line and sinker, and over 400,000 nippers were 'freed' to loving homes, along with accompanying merchandise like digital watches (the up-to-the-minute technology!) and T-shirts. Clever little nippers.

Fungie the Dolphin

From 1983, this famed bottlenose dolphin was often to be found swimming off the coast of Dingle, and a thriving boat-tour industry was built up around his frequent appearances in the harbour. After greeting a whole generation of fishermen on their journeys back home, Fungie finally went quiet in 2020 – as suddenly as he had arrived. Despite a series of searches, the much-loved dolphin is presumed to have gone to that big harbour in the sky. Ar dheis Dé go raibh a anam.

G

Gaeilge

When Irish became an official working language of the EU in 2005, we all cheered with patriotic pride at the long-awaited recognition of our native tongue. Now, 'An bhfuil cead agam dul go dtí an leithreas, más é do thoil é?'

Game of Thrones

Filmed in spectacularly beautiful areas of Northern Ireland, *Game of Thrones* had fans from around the globe flocking to Ulster to see locations from their favourite show, even causing traffic chaos on the Dark Hedges (aka the Kingsroad). The most illegally downloaded show in the world, *GoT* had it all: a gripping storyline, high production values, award-winning acting and a healthy helping of gratuitous nudity. Let's just all try and forget THAT story finale.

Garth Brooks

Hey, he didn't mean to cause a big scene, but that's exactly what happened in 2014, when the world's biggest country star announced he was coming to play Croke Park. Demand was phenomenal, and two concerts became three, and then five, with 400,000 tickets sold. Problem was, Croke Park had a licence for only three gigs a year, and all three already belonged to One Direction. A compromise of three nights was offered to Garth, but for him it was five or nothing – and all the gigs were cancelled. A sad year for Irish Stetsons.

Gay Byrne Pranked

In an episode of *The Live Mike* in 1982, Gay Byrne was set up to deliver a live piece to camera in the grounds of Trinity College. Up comes Mike Murphy, Gay's colleague and friend, ridiculously dressed as a French football fan and constantly interrupting. The famously cool and clean-spoken *Late Late* host finally lost it and asked the obnoxious Frenchman, 'Do you understand the expression to f**k off?' The show went down a storm, and Gay's candid reaction only made the Irish public love him even more.

Good Friday

From 1927 to 2017, Irish pubs were strictly forbidden from opening their doors on Good Friday every year. That meant one thing: people shopping for alcohol on Holy Thursday like the world was going to end and all we had left to do was party. That finally changed in 2018, the first year the pubs could legally open on Good Friday. And then Covid-19 happened, which roundly put one day of pub closures into perspective.

Grafton Street Pedestrianisation

Traffic on Dublin's Grafton Street in the 1960s was a nightmare, so pedestrianisation was first trialled there for four weeks in 1971. It took another decade before it was officially made a pedestrian street, on 1 December 1982, and it was a huge success. Looking at the Brown Thomas Christmas window wouldn't be quite as enjoyable with bumper-to-bumper cars behind you. And where would all the buskers go?

Grand National Glory

In 2021 Rachael Blackmore raised the spirits of a locked-down nation when she became the first-ever woman jockey to win the Grand National. Aboard Minella Times, the Tipperary native stormed across the finishing line, smashing gender stereotypes in her wake.

Grand Slam Victory

The Irish had managed to notch up some Triple Crowns (beating England, Scotland and Wales in the rugby Six

Nations) in the early 2000s, but when the country finally won its first Grand Slam (beating bleedin' everyone) in sixty-one years, the place went absolutely wild. It was 2009, the final match was against Wales in Cardiff, and there were just two points between us when the final whistle blew. Ronan O'Gara's drop goal in the closing minutes was pure class. *chef's kiss*

Great Balls of Fire

In February 2010, a meteorite exploded at an altitude of 100 miles, creating a huge fireball and sending fragments of rock crashing into our atmosphere – with reports of some landing in Co. Cavan. We were all so panicked trying to find out if we were being invaded by UFOs that we crashed the Astronomy Ireland website. Steady.

Green Shield Stamps

All the rage in the 1970s, Green Shield stamps were an offshoot of the British scheme, with a distribution centre they called 'a modern Aladdin's cave, magically transported to Clondalkin'. Stamps were earned by spending at local shops and petrol stations, and kids often jostled for position to be the one to lick and stick the stamps – nice and straight, now. Looking through the glossy catalogues, hopes were high of getting enough stamps to bring home a TV (375 books full of 1,280 stamps each) or a washing machine (185 books), but – let's face it – most of us had to settle for a set of mugs.

Gripe Water

For generations of Irish parents, gripe water was the answer to all their prayers. The mix of sodium bicarb, dill oil, sugar and just a smidge (up to 9%, actually) of alcohol worked wonders on fussy and colicky babies, sending them off to blissful sleep. When the alcohol content was eventually banned here in 2005, people were known to go to great lengths to get their hands on contraband from Northern Ireland or England. But bless them, they were only thinking of the children.

H

Hall's Pictorial Weekly

RTÉ's flagship comedy programme in the 1970s, with satirical sketches written by Frank Hall and featuring characters like Cha and Miah, the Minister for Hardship, and Frank Kelly's local councillor with his Ballymagash-style politics. It lampooned everything from songs to TV programmes but especially politics, even being credited with the downfall of the Fine Gael–Labour government in 1977. That's what you call sharp-tongued satire.

Hand of Henry

The blatant handball by French striker Thierry Henry during the second leg of the qualifiers that robbed Ireland of our rightful place in the 2010 FIFA World Cup. Fans were so incensed that they even protested outside the French Embassy in Dublin. Never forgive, never forget.

Henri Hippo

Back in the 1980s, Ulster Bank knew the best way to get customers was to catch 'em young. Children who joined their junior savings club were the happy recipients of a Henri Hippo money box, as well as goodies like wallets and calendars. The character was resurrected in 2008, in a bid by Ulster Bank to get nostalgic parents to pass on the saving habit to their own children – but 2008 wasn't really the best time to start investing anywhere. Least of all the banks.

Hole in the Wall

In February 1980, Bank of Ireland introduced Ireland's first-ever ATM. It was situated in Stillorgan, Co. Dublin, and required a Pass card and four-digit PIN to retrieve money from your account – the thrill! There are now over 3,000 ATMs around the country and the average withdrawal is €130 per transaction. Cha-ching!

Holy Hour

Introduced in the 1920s, all pubs in the country were obliged to observe a 'holy hour' by closing between 2pm and 4pm every Sunday. That tradition stood until it was finally abolished in 2000. Not that many pubs saw a huge difference, to be fair – they just didn't shut their doors, turn off the lights and pretend no one was home on a Sunday afternoon.

Home to Vote

Fair play to anyone who managed to hold back the tears when #HomeToVote began trending on 21 May 2015, the day thousands of Irish expats tweeted their journeys home for the marriage equality referendum. And three years later, #HomeToVote trended once again as the Irish returned home in droves to vote on the Eighth Amendment.

'Horse Outside'

This expletive-laden rap by Limerick comedy duo The Rubberbandits was released in December 2010, peaking at No 2 for Christmas and racking up more than twenty million views on YouTube. The video showed a lucky bridesmaid being serenaded by the plastic bag-sporting bandits in their attempts to persuade her to choose their preferred mode of transport – for a more exciting ride.

Hot Priest

Irish actor Andrew Scott set groins alight in his role as the 'Hot Priest' in the BBC comedy *Fleabag*, written by and starring Phoebe Waller-Bridge. The world just could not get enough of the brewing sexual tension between Fleabag and the ordained object of her affection, with related internet searches jumping by 160%. For anyone out there still carrying a torch for the 'Hot Priest', just remember the wise words from the man himself: 'It'll pass.' Amen.

How Do They Get the Figs into the Fig Rolls?

With the whole country captivated by the question for decades, this Jacob's campaign was an ad executive's dream. The original idea had Jim Figgerty, private detective, protecting the secret formula from sneaky thieves, but it evolved over the years to have cartoon kids pontificating about whether it was done by aliens or magical elves. And how do they actually get the figs in? It involves a mountain of mushed-up figs, a machine called an extruder and, honest to God, you don't want to know.

How Do You Do?

Back in the late 1980s/early 1990s, Mary Fitzgerald's RTÉ show *How Do You Do?* was as exciting as it got. Given a pile of empty toilet rolls, an egg box, some pipe cleaners, crêpe paper and a tube of glitter glue, there was nothing she couldn't make. A spaceship? A doll's house? A selection of papier mâché fruit and vegetables? The woman was the MacGyver of the arts and crafts world.

Hurling on Sky Sports

When Sky Sports broadcast their first hurling match in
2014, the response from first-time watchers was hilarious,
with the Brits trying to keep track of the fast-moving
sliotar and – with all that clash of the ash – wondering
how any hurlers were left alive afterwards. They asked
some sensible questions too: How's the goalie supposed to
save a ball going over the bar? Why isn't he wearing any
padding for protection? And without a glove to be seen,
do the hurlers all have fingers like steel?

Hurricane Higgins

Twice World Snooker Champion and iconic player
throughout the 1970s and 1980s – just when the
sport was starting to attract some serious TV ratings –
Belfast's Alex 'Hurricane' Higgins was famous for his
fast, attacking play. Who can forget the image of him
in tears, World Championship trophy in one hand and
his baby in the other, after that 135 break against Ray
Reardon in the final frame of the '82 final? A much-
loved people's champion, his nickname also owed
something to his volatile personality – not just a man
but a force of nature.

I

In the Name of the Father

Starring our very own Daniel Day-Lewis as Gerry Conlon, Jim Sheridan's film told the story of the Guildford Four and the Maguire Seven, their wrongful convictions and their eventual exoneration after a lengthy legal battle. When Day-Lewis delivered the line 'I'm a free man, and I'm going out the front door!', people watching it in cinemas here couldn't help themselves, standing, clapping and cheering to see justice finally done. I'm not crying, you're crying.

Iodine Tablets

The Irish government distributed iodine tablets to all households in 2002, for use in the event of a nuclear emergency – with an eye to a possible accident at or terror attack on the plants in Sellafield or Chapelcross. Those iodine tablets had a shelf life of about three years, expiring in 2005, so if you still have them at the back of a cupboard, now might be the time to throw them away.

Ireland Fans

Ireland fans have long had a reputation for being up for the craic and magnanimous in both victory and defeat, and nowhere was this more evident than on the streets of France during the Euros in 2016. Videos popped up all over the internet of our fans serenading babies on the train, charming the gendarmes and generally being sound. For their good humour and exemplary sportsmanship, they were awarded the Medal of the City of Paris. The Ireland team? Scraped into the knockout stages. Irish fans? World beaters.

'Ireland's Call'

Commissioned by the IRFU for the 1995 Rugby World Cup, Phil Coulter's anthem was written for use where the Ireland team is one that includes the entire island, all four provinces. Later adopted by other sports, like hockey and cricket, there is a grudging acceptance of it by fans who were reared on 'Amhrán na bhFiann'. But you'll hear it belted out full force anytime there's a Triple Crown or a Grand Slam in the offing.

Ireland vs New Zealand

There was a lot of crowing done when Ireland beat the All Blacks in 2016, but it was our women's team who were first to beat the mighty New Zealand. Incredibly, the Black Ferns hadn't lost a World Cup game since 1991 when Ireland handed them a 17–14 defeat at the 2014 World Cup – showing the lads how it's done.

The Irish Press

First published in 1931, the *Irish Press* newspaper was founded by Éamon de Valera to support Fianna Fáil, with Margaret Pearse, mother of Patrick and Willie, pushing the button to start the presses. It ran for more than sixty years, but closed with debts of £20 million and the loss of 600 jobs, with its last-ever edition published in May 1995. No longer would the streets of Dublin ring out with the bizarre-sounding, run-together phrase 'HerdledorPress!'

Italia '90

Ireland's first-ever World Cup, when the country became Jack's Army and 'Olé, Olé, Olé, Olé!' and 'Put 'Em Under Pressure!' could be heard everywhere. Drawing our way through the group stages, and then Packie's save and David O'Leary's penalty and a quarter-final place. Celebrations spilling onto the streets and unbelievable national pride. Best summer ever.

I Think I'm Going Back ...

Alan Hughes' hair will forever hold a place in our hearts
for its part in this ESB ad from 1988. To the haunting
melody of Dusty Springfield's 'Goin' Back', Alan arrives
back in his hometown – met at the train station by his
beloved daddy. As they drive home and night falls, Alan
stares out the car window, pondering all the electricity
that his mammy is using to prepare for his return. And
forget the electric blanket, the final seconds – when
he runs into his mammy's arms – will warm even the
coldest heart.

'I Useta Lover'

The Saw Doctors' first hit, this 1990 single shot to No 1
and stayed there for nine weeks, becoming one of the
best-selling Irish singles of all time. The folk-rock number
captured the nation with its up-tempo beat and catchy
lyrics about a crush on a mass-going, Concern-fasting gal a
long, long time ago. Sure, we've all been there.

J

Jedward

The giddy, coiffed singing duo, identical twins John and Edward Grimes, took the world by storm when they appeared on *The X-Factor* in 2009. Everyone laughed at first, then watched in astonishment as their two albums went platinum, they competed in both the Eurovision and *Celebrity Big Brother* (not once but twice) and accrued a combined personal worth of about €6 million. Quiff-tastic.

Joe Brolly

No stranger to controversy, the former Derry footballer and *Sunday Game* pundit really kicked things off after the 2013 quarter-final between Tyrone and Monaghan. In what was called the 'rant of the year', he angrily attacked the Tyrone team's style of play, accusing them of cynical fouls. The media got great mileage from it before it eventually blew over. Just a bit of a storm in the Sam Maguire cup.

'Jumbo Breakfast Roll'

Pat Shortt's fast-singing, oh-so-catchy ode to his favourite breakfast: a full Irish on a demi-baguette, wrapped up good and tight. Ireland's best-selling single of 2006, it hit the No 1 slot and kept it for six weeks, outselling Shakira's 'Hips Don't Lie' and Justin Timberlake's 'SexyBack'. Can you believe that? I can in me roll.

Junior Cert

The Junior Cert was first introduced as the successor to the Inter Cert for first years in 1989, with its inaugural exams taking place in 1992. Best test of someone's age is which of them they sat: if you're Inter and they're Junior, they're just not going to get your jokes.

Just a Minute Quiz

The long-running radio quiz with the much-missed Larry Gogan gave us some comedy gold over the years, with panicked guesses from contestants up against the clock. From 'F' being the capital of France, to 'Heil' being Hitler's first name, and the Taj Mahal being located 'opposite the dental hospital'. Ah, they just didn't suit you.

K

Katie Taylor's Olympic Gold

The trailblazing boxer was Ireland's flag bearer at the 2012 London Olympics, with the hopes of a nation on her shoulders. And she didn't disappoint. Her final against Russian Sofya Ochigava on 9 August was watched at home by 1.1 million people, with even more tuned in in bars and offices around the country and all over the world. When Katie was presented with her gold medal, the ecstatic Irish fans in the ExCeL Arena absolutely lifted the roof. We could hear them from over here.

Kellie Harrington

And there were more emotional scenes during the postponed Tokyo Olympics in 2021 when Dubliner Kellie Harrington brought home yet another boxing gold for Ireland. Following the performance of a lifetime, Harrington said she felt the whole country behind her as she heroically defeated the reigning world champion. A class act.

Kerbs

The street game of the 1980s, Kerbs was played across roads up and down the country. Players took turns to bounce a ball off the opposite kerb, earning points depending on the difficulty of the throw. On a warm summer's day, local championships could go on for hours – or at least until you were called in for your tea.

Kerrygold Ads

Back in the 1990s, when ads were like soap operas, we were all hooked on the Kerrygold saga. No one was quite sure what was going on, but one plot involved a woman cooking the dinner under the watchful eye of a French fisherman, and another a wistful Irish farmer selling a French woman a horse. But did hunky André put a bit of butter on the spuds? And just who did take the horse to France?

Kim & Kanye Honeymoon

Their marriage may not have stood the test of time, but it sure got off to a great start. Kimye flew into Cork Airport, stayed in a castle and went to the cinema in Portlaoise and Tullamore. Trip of a lifetime.

Knock Airport

Ireland West Airport in Mayo was the dream of

Monsignor James Horan, part of his plan to attract even more pilgrims to the nearby Holy Shrine at Knock. It was officially opened in 1986, after a long and controversial campaign by the Monsignor and overcoming the logistics of building anything smack-bang in the middle of a bog. Thank God for a soft landing.

Krispy Kreme

When the US doughnut chain opened their first Irish outlet in Blanchardstown in 2018, they couldn't have anticipated the reaction. Demand was so high that queues of cars snaked back from the drive-through, with drivers honking horns in excited anticipation at all hours of the day and night. It was like Dubliners had never before tasted deep-fried dough.

L

Lacrosse

Having qualified to play at the 2022 World Games in Alabama, the Irish lacrosse team knew that the Iroquois Nationals, a Native American team, had failed to secure a place only because they're not recognised as a sovereign nation – despite the fact that the modern lacrosse game actually originated with them. The Irish stepped up and offered to let the Iroquois compete in their place, saying it was 'the right thing to do'. Well played, Ireland. Well played.

Lansdowne Road Carpet

It was 2003, and Ireland and England were going head-to-head at Lansdowne Road to claim the Grand Slam that year. In what was seen as a sign of disrespect, England captain Martin Johnson and his team lined up in the wrong place before the anthems, forcing Irish President Mary McAleese to walk off her red carpet to greet them. The Ireland team faltered that day, but not our President, who gamely marched onto the grass without missing a beat.

Leaving Cert Leak

There were all sorts of ructions around the 2009 Leaving Cert, when the second English paper was accidentally distributed to students instead of the first paper in a Drogheda school – with several eagle-eyed students spotting the mistake. Word of the leak soon spread on chat forums and social media, and without time to distribute the back-up contingency Paper II, there was no alternative but to reschedule the exam for the Saturday. There go the weekend plans.

Let There Be (Environmentally Friendly) Light

Ireland was the first country in the world to ban the traditional lightbulb, with 2009 legislation phasing them out and ushering in new long-life bulbs. And after a bit of grumbling, we soon adjusted to the wait time needed before you can actually see anything.

Life of Brian

With such staunch Catholicism the status quo for so long, it's no wonder that we have a chequered history of censoring the arts. One film that fell afoul of the censor was the comedy classic *Monty Python's Life of Brian.* Banned on its release in 1979 for mocking the Christian faith, it remained that way for another eight years, with under-the-counter pirate VHS tapes the only way of finding out what all the fuss was about. Blessed be the dodgy video shops.

Line Dancing

A national obsession in 1990s Ireland, community halls and hotel function rooms were packed to the rafters with men and women hitting their heels and cowboy-shuffling across the floor. Even the likes of Colin Farrell got in on the act, with damning photographic evidence to prove it. Scary while it lasted, the moment passed and line dancing grapevined back to Middle America, where it belonged.

Live Aid

On Saturday, 13 July 1985, the global music event organised by Bob Geldof and Midge Ure took place to raise funds for famine relief in Ethiopia. Two concerts were staged in London and Philadelphia, with 1.9 billion people (over a third of the planet) tuning in to watch on TV. Ireland was the biggest per-capita donor during the event, with £7 million. During the live broadcast, when the BBC presenter wanted to give viewers a list of addresses for donations, Geldof broke in with 'F**k the address, let's get the [phone] numbers!' Donations swiftly increased to £300 per second, and the Irish were never so proud.

Lost Caravaggio

In August 1990, an original Caravaggio was discovered in one of the houses of the Jesuit Fathers on Leeson Street, Dublin. The painting had been gifted to the community in the 1930s, in gratitude for spiritual guidance, little knowing that it was an original by the Italian master, 'The Taking of Christ'. Now on indefinite loan to the National Gallery, you can go and see what €50 million buys you these days.

Love/Hate

The hit Dublin crime drama that kept a million viewers on tenterhooks for five seasons. Of all the shocking moments – and there were many – nothing received such a response as when Wayne, the baby-faced criminal, turned his machine gun on a cat. There was uproar. But viewers were assured that no animals were harmed in the making.

M

M50

Launched to great fanfare in 2005, the M50 was designed to take commuters from one side of the capital to the other with ease. But despite three decades of planning, building, upgrades and the introduction of barrier-free tolling, you'll still find yourself sitting bumper-to-bumper on grey and gloomy lanes in bank-holiday traffic. Sit back and crank up the radio.

Mallow Airport

In 1983, a fifteen-seater Gulfstream jet was forced to make an unexpected landing at Mallow Racecourse. Captain Ruben Ocaña and his Mexican crew were stranded in the Cork town for thirty-nine days while a makeshift runway was built, but the locals made them very welcome – even roping the captain into judging a local beauty contest. Ocaña returned the following year with his family. No emergency landing required that time.

'Maniac 2000'

The anthem of a generation. This banger of a tune by Mark McCabe had teenagers and twenty-somethings packing dance floors across the country, belting out the lyrics while jumping around like their lives depended on it. One simple question to answer: Are. You. Ready?!

Mary Robinson

In December 1990, Mary Robinson became the first woman President of Ireland and shook things up from the very beginning. The Mayo native had a reputation as an equal rights campaigner, and she revolutionised and reinvigorated what had previously been seen as just a ceremonial role. In her acceptance speech she praised 'mná na hÉireann, who instead of rocking the cradle rocked the system' and made us all believe that we could make a difference. Mnásome.

Matt Damon

When the coronavirus hit in 2020, Oscar-winner Matt Damon and his family were locked down in the coastal town of Dalkey. The locals had a great time snapping candid pics of him, including down at the Vico with his swimming towel tucked away in a SuperValu bag. A-lister endorsement for your neighbourhood supermarket: what a coup!

Mattie Bán

When the long-awaited *Friends* reunion happened in May 2021, Irish Twitter blew up with comparisons of Matt LeBlanc to Irish daddies and uncles everywhere. The image of him sitting on the couch, arms crossed, was captioned with classic Da lines and photoshopped convincingly into everywhere from *The Sunday Game* panel to the *Late Late Show* audience. #HowYouGettinOn

Metric Conversion

In 2005, all Irish road signs were changed from imperial to metric, in line with our European partners. About 36,000 destination distance signs needed changing, and 23,000 brand new speed-limit signs were erected. For older drivers, who'd been using miles all their lives, it was a massive change. Sure, some of them are only just getting used to the kilometres now.

Millennium Clock

Oh, we were all very excited about celebrating a new millennium. So much so that someone thought it would be a good idea to put a digital clock in the notoriously grimy River Liffey in Dublin city, counting down the minutes and hours to the year 2000. The six-tonne, £250,000 clock languished beneath the murky waters and became known as 'The Time in the Slime'. A few months later, it was taken from the river and written off as a very bad idea.

Mná na hÉireann

First female Aer Lingus pilot: Gráinne Cronin, 1977.
First modern female government minister: Máire Geoghegan-Quinn, 1979.
First female high court judge: Mella Carroll, 1980.
First female president: Mary Robinson, 1990.
First female Church of Ireland bishop: Pat Storey, 2013.
Still no sign of her Catholic counterpart.

Molly Malone

A statue of Molly Malone, the heroine of the famous Irish ballad, was unveiled at the bottom of Grafton Street as part of the city's millennium celebrations in 1988 and proved popular with photo-snapping tourists and locals alike. Fifteen years later, she had to make way for Luas works so has since wheeled her wheelbarrow around the corner to Suffolk Street.

Moneygall

In May 2011, American President Barack Obama and First Lady Michelle visited Moneygall as part of their trip to Ireland. They were greeted by thousands of cheering locals, including the President's eighth cousin, Henry Healy, who had helped trace Obama's roots to the small Offaly town. More than a century after Obama's ancestors escaped the Irish Famine for New York, the future President was born and the American dream fully realised. Even more so when Pat McDonagh opened up a new service station on the outskirts of Moneygall and named it Barack Obama Plaza.

Moone Boy

Chris O'Dowd's hilariously bittersweet sitcom was based on his experience of growing up in the small rural town of Boyle, Co. Roscommon, in the 1990s. With Chris himself as the very tall imaginary friend of local boy Martin Moone, the show features cameo appearances from a rake of Irish actors including Amy Huberman, Sharon Horgan, Bressie and Limerick legend Terry Wogan. Even Hollywood star Paul Rudd makes an appearance. Roscommon didn't know what hit it.

Moving Statues

Ah, the summer of 1985, when people flocked in their droves to more than thirty villages countrywide in the wake of widespread sightings of moving statues of the Virgin Mary and other saintly figures. Rumour had it that by rubbing a handkerchief on one of these statues you could bring back some of their divine power to a loved one at home. Best present ever.

Mrs. Brown's Boys

Comedian Brendan O'Carroll could never be accused of overnight success – he has been working on the character of Agnes Brown since 1992. *Mrs. Brown's Boys* started life as a radio play before becoming a series of books, a Hollywood film featuring Anjelica Huston, an onstage show and then its most successful incarnation: a sitcom watched and loved by millions around the world. As Mrs. Brown herself would say, 'That's nice'. *with a sideways glance to camera*

MT-USA

Back in 1984, in a time before music streaming and YouTube, MT-USA was like nothing Irish viewers had seen before. Presented by 'Fab' Vincent Hanley – all the way from New York! – it was Ireland's first music video programme and the show to tune in to for the latest US releases, music news and interviews. It was Ireland's answer to MTV – back when MTV used to actually play music.

Munster vs All Blacks

Tuesday, 31 October 1978 was a day that rocked the rugby world, with the victory of Munster over the legendary New Zealand All Blacks: a 12–0 scoreline in front of a crowd of 12,000 in Thomond Park, with hundreds more fans sitting on the twenty-foot-high wall and still others in the trees outside or watching from windows of local houses. During the match, the atmosphere was electric – at the final whistle, absolute elation.

Music, Maestro

Eimear Noone is the award-winning Galwegian conductor and composer of musical scores for video games like 'World of Warcraft' and 'The Legend of Zelda'. She made history in 2020 when she became the first woman to conduct the orchestra at the Oscars. Bravo!

My Friend, Totò

He destroyed the dreams of an Irish nation when his goal ended Ireland's phenomenal time at the 1990 World Cup. But when Salvatore 'Totò' Schillaci turned up in a Smithwick's ad, we almost forgave him. After all, 'It was a good goal'.

My Left Foot

The 1989 biopic of Christy Brown, an Irishman with severe cerebral palsy, only able to control his eponymous left foot. At what was one of the best nights ever for the Irish at the Oscars, Brenda Fricker took home the gong for Best Supporting Actress and Daniel Day-Lewis the Best Actor. And the Irish nation adopted Day-Lewis as one of our own for the rest of his days.

'My Lovely Horse'

Written by The Divine Comedy, this song featured in a classic episode of *Father Ted* when it was Ted and Dougal's entry for the Eurosong Contest. With all the showering with sugar lumps and those fetlocks blowing in the wind, it was so catchy that the pair nearly went all the way with it too. In fairness, it was a better offering than Dustin's 'Irelande Douze Pointe'.

N

Nadine Coyle's Passport

Possibly one of the most cringe-inducing moments on Irish television: when Nadine Coyle was caught lying on *Popstars* about her age in order to secure a place in Ireland's newest pop band, Six. Being unceremoniously booted from the show and the band turned out to be for the best; Nadine went on to win a place in one of the world's biggest girl bands, Girls Aloud, and toured the world with that infamous passport in tow.

National Lottery

Ireland's first-ever National Lottery millionaire, Rita Power from Co. Galway, pocketed a handy £1.2 million in 1989. Never ones to have their heads turned, Rita and husband John Joe, who owned just ten cows at the time of their win, opted to quietly share their money with family. They didn't even trade in their car, keeping their trusted Ford Fiesta for years afterwards. Probably sprang for a more regular oil change, though.

Nice Referendum

Ireland was the only EU member state to hold public referendums on the Nice Treaty. The first vote was rejected by a narrow margin in 2001. However, a year later, the powers that be made us have a do-over, and this time the treaty, which would allow for expansion of the EU, was ratified. If only they'd taken a similar approach with Brexit ...

Nighthawks

Broadcast on Network 2 three nights a week from 1988 to 1992, *Nighthawks* had Shay Healy interviewing a variety of guests in a makeshift bar with a smoky and relaxed atmosphere. So relaxed, in fact, that former Justice Minister Sean Doherty casually revealed that several people within Taoiseach Charlie Haughey's cabinet were aware of the tapping of journalists' phones in the early 1980s. A day later, Haughey announced his intention to resign. Now that's good TV.

Nightlife

When it came to Dublin nightlife, The Pink Elephant was the place for celebs to be seen in the 1980s. As the Celtic Tiger began to roar, The Kitchen, Reynards and Lillie's Bordello – with their burly bouncers and strict door policies – were all vying to be the new hotspot in town. In the days before mobile phones and social media, these exclusive clubs were frequented by boy-band members, models and visiting celebs, partying Dublin-style. The rest of us headed to Coppers, then on to Leggs on Leeson Street for a £30 bottle of Liebfraumilch.

'No, no, no, no, no, no, no, no, no, no, no'

The Rose of Tralee is renowned for many things – not least the hip-hop dance routine from Dublin Rose Siobhéal Nic Eochaidh – but how could we forget that infamous proposal on stage? When her boyfriend got down on one knee and asked Molly Molloy Gambel, the 2013 New Orleans Rose, to marry him, she said no, over and over, again and again, but later assured people that it was because she was in shock. The following year, the happy bride did, in fact, go on to say YES!

Normal People

Based on Sally Rooney's book, this steamy TV adaptation had the whole country talking. The story of the relationship between Connell and Marianne as they move from secondary school in rural Ireland to university in the Big Smoke featured a number of sex scenes, including the longest one ever aired on Irish television. We all went wild for Kildare native Paul Mescal, whose character's

O'Neills GAA shorts saw a 20% bump in sales, and his gold chain even got its own Instagram account. #madeit

'Nothing Compares 2 U'

Written by Prince, this beautiful song about lost love was released by Sinéad O'Connor in 1990 and is memorable as much for her performance in the video, a full-face close-up as she sings the heartbreaking lyrics, a single tear rolling down each cheek. ALL the feels.

O

Offaly denies Kerry Five-in-a-Row

The 1982 All-Ireland football final has gone down in the history books for one of the most famous GAA moments of all time. Kerry needed to beat Offaly to secure a historic five-in-a-row, but it was an unexpected last-minute goal from sub Séamus Darby – in his only kick of the match – that clinched it for Offaly and dashed all of Kerry's dreams. Even now, mention of the name Séamus Darby is enough to trigger PTSD in many a Kerry fan.

Oliver Plunkett

In the 1670s, when the English government's anti-Catholic sentiment was at its most dangerous, Archbishop Oliver Plunkett continued to travel the countryside dressed as a layman, tending to his people. He was eventually caught, tried as a traitor and executed. Centuries later, in 1975, he was canonised – the first new Irish saint for seven hundred years. Now his preserved head rests in a shrine in a Drogheda church. Did somebody say 'the perfect school tour'?

Oscar Speeches

In 2008, Glen Hansard and Markéta Irglová won the

Oscar for Best Original Song for their beautiful ballad 'Falling Slowly' from the film *Once*. Glen Hansard gave a fitting, self-deprecating speech, but just as Markéta took to the microphone to speak, the music played her off. The Oscars host, Jon Stewart, brought Markéta back out on stage where she delivered a heartfelt speech encouraging independent artists to dream big.

Oscar Wilde Statue

It took us nearly a century after he died, but in 1997 we finally commemorated one of Ireland's most-loved poets and playwrights with a statue by sculptor Danny Osborne in Dublin's Merrion Square. Wilde's figure relaxes on a rock, wearing a very dapper green and pink smoking jacket and an enigmatic expression that often proves a talking point. And as the man himself once said, 'There is only one thing in life worse than being talked about, and that is not being talked about.'

P

Pandas

In 1986, Chinese pandas Ming Ming and Ping Ping were seen outside their home country for the very first time when they arrived at Dublin Zoo, on loan. The cuddly black and white bears spent a hundred days at the zoo posing for pictures and delighting the children of Ireland (and their parents too!).

Passports for Sale

There was a time in Ireland when investors could quite literally buy an Irish passport. For a decade up until 1998, a ridiculously wealthy applicant – who may or may not have been trying to reduce their tax bill elsewhere – only had to make a one-off investment of £1,000,000, and ninety days later the government would hand them over an Irish passport and a 'Céad Míle Fáilte'.

Pelé at Dalymount

In 1972, Irish soccer fans' dreams came true when they got to see one of the world's top footballers, Pelé, play in Dalymount Park with his club side Santos FC. The Brazilians beat a selection of players from Bohemians and Drumcondra 3–2, but much to the disappointment of the 27,500 spectators who'd forked out the £2 to see him, Pelé didn't even score. Not a good game, and not a great game either.

'Penney's Gotta Whole Lotta Things for Christmas'

Originally broadcast in the 1980s, this iconic Penney's ad has had many iterations but is undoubtedly the most memorable Christmas jingle of all time. And very difficult to get out of your head. Bet you're singing it right now ...

Penny Sweets

Remember the days when ten pence could get you an enviable selection of sugary goodness? Fizzy cola bottles, milk teeth, flying saucers, jelly worms, sour soothers, white mice filled with pink goo, blackjacks, fruit salads, applejacks and jazzy discs all crammed together in a white plastic bag. Makes your teeth ache just thinking about it.

People in Need

Ireland's first-ever telethon was held in 1989 and was the single biggest operation that RTÉ had hosted on its own. Fronted by Gay Byrne, it was a huge success, raising

£2.3 million for Irish charities. But what is a telethon, I hear younger readers ask. Well, before we could text our charitable donations, we used to have to phone them in or even visit a local bank and lodge them by hand. How mad is that?!

Peter Casey

Peter Casey could not have been happier when his horse, Flemenstar, ridden by Andrew Lynch, took the top position at Leopardstown in 2012. In an interview with RTÉ's Tracy Piggott, the excited trainer let everyone know that Flemenstar wouldn't be the only one getting a ride that day!

Pint Baby

A viral sensation in 2017, Pint Baby was a babe-in-arms spotted supping from his mammy's pint in a 1997 episode of *Nationwide* recorded in an Ennistymon pub. The country was captivated by this precocious little stout-swiller and determined to track him down. Turns out, Pint Baby has grown up into a fine Kildare lad, and that little tipple did him no harm at all. *Health & safety warning: please don't try this at home.*

The Ploughing

The National Ploughing Championships have been going strong since 1931 and now take place over three days, with nearly 300,000 visitors roaming over seven hundred acres of field. Popular competitions include brown bread-baking, sheep-shearing, cow milking and, of course, welly throwing. All very thirsty work, and around 60,000 cups of tea and coffee and 16,000 litres of milk are drunk over the three days. In 2015, they poured 1,848 cups of tea in one hour – a Guinness World Record!

Pound Coin

In 1990, Ireland replaced the £1 note when it started issuing the first pound coins, featuring the distinctive red deer native to Ireland. You could get a whole lot of 10p bags and bars with one of those silver coins, which were just *made* for being slipped into your hand by Granny or Granddad.

President Higgins's Dogs

It was rare to see footage of the President in the Áras without his trusty Burmese mountain dogs, Síoda and Bród, by his side. So the nation was heartbroken when it heard of the death of Síoda in 2020. But six months later, heartbreak turned to excitement when the President welcomed a new furry ball of joy, Misneach, into his home. Is there anything cuter than a new puppy?

P.S. I Love You

In 2004, Cecelia Ahern published her debut novel *P.S. I Love You*. The twenty-two-year-old daughter of Taoiseach Bertie Ahern had received one of the biggest advances in publishing history – and a movie deal to boot. Her critics were dubious, but she went on to prove them wrong by selling two million copies – and writing more than a dozen other novels with combined sales of over twenty-five million copies. P.S. She showed them.

'Pull Like a Dog'

This handy little phrase came from silver medal rowers Gary and Paul O'Donovan at the 2016 Rio Olympics. The Skibbereen brothers won the hearts of the nation and became an overnight sensation with their laid-back interview technique when Paul summed up rowing with: 'It isn't too complex really. A to B as fast as you can go and hope for the best. Close the eyes and pull like a dog.' Paul went on to clinch gold at the Tokyo Olympics in 2021 with rowing partner Fintan McCarthy, so he's definitely doing something right!

Q

Quake!

The largest earthquake ever to hit Ireland was in 1984, recording a 5.5 on the Richter scale. Many heard the tell-tale rumble when buildings along the east of the country shook, but only the odd structural crack or fallen chimney was reported. And hardly a dustbin knocked over.

Queen Elizabeth *as Gaeilge*

At a state dinner held in her honour in Dublin Castle in 2011, Queen Elizabeth II began her speech with the words 'A Uachtaráin, agus a chairde'. President McAleese was openly surprised and impressed to hear the British monarch using the Irish language. As were most of the guests. You could almost hear a whispered 'Gabh mo leithscéal?' echo through the room.

Queen of Ireland

An important symbol of modern Ireland and a highly influential figure in the 2015 marriage equality referendum, Panti Bliss gave it socks with her 'Noble Call' at the Abbey Theatre in 2014, when she called for an end to homophobia and equal rights for all. It was a powerful speech, which was listened to by millions the world over and really helped effect change. Truly inspirational!

Quoting Mícheál Ó Muircheartaigh

For six decades, Mícheál Ó Muircheartaigh gifted us
with his legendary GAA commentary. There was no one
who could bring a match to life for listeners quite like
the Kerry broadcaster. And we can never get enough
of his quotes, from his Rabbitte chasing a Fox around
Croke Park, to neither Fermanagh nor Fiji being hurling
strongholds, to not a big man or a small man but a handy
man. Every single one a classic.

R

Rainbow Coalitions

We've had a bit of experience with rainbow coalitions in Irish politics. Sadly, not as much fun as they sound.

'Rat Trap'

Once upon a time there was a Boomtown Rat and a turkey … Dustin the Turkey started life on classic RTÉ children's show *The Den* with Ray D'Arcy and Zig and Zag, and went on to become one of Ireland's most prolific '90s music acts. He had four successful albums and managed to convince a host of Irish artists to collaborate with him including Joe Dolan, Linda Martin, Christy Dignam and even Bob Geldof. For many '90s kids the lyrics of 'Rat Trap' will forever be 'Geldof, take a wash, take a wash…'

Ray Houghton's Header

One of the most momentous goals in the history of Irish football. Ray Houghton will go down in history for THAT famous header against the old enemy, England, during Euro '88. Altogether now: 'Who put the ball in the English net?'

The Riordans

RTÉ's landmark drama *The Riordans* ran from 1965 to 1979 and was set on a family farm in Co. Kilkenny, with stars like Gabriel Byrne and Biddy White Lennon. A huge hit with viewers, both the cast and audience were taken by surprise by RTÉ's decision to axe the show at the height of its popularity. But for head writer Wesley Burrowes even bigger success would beckon – with a little soap called *Glenroe*.

Riverdance

Will we ever forget that moment when Jean Butler and Michael Flatley took to the stage during the Eurovision in Dublin's Point Theatre in 1994? It was positively spine-tingling. The massive cheer that erupted from the audience at the performance's conclusion said it all. Riverdance went on to become one of the most successful dance productions in the world and now even has its own animation – with Pierce Brosnan and Brendan Gleeson voicing, no less!

Roller Skates

Roller skates were *the* things to be seen wearing in 1980s

Ireland. Kids skated everywhere, with not an elbow or knee pad in sight! And there was no greater fun on earth than a roller-skating disco. Later came rollerblades, health and safety, and correctly fitted protective equipment – those '90s kids weren't quite as hardy as the '80s ones.

Roll in the Hay

Well, Holy God, but was the Irish nation ever more shocked than when Miley went for a roll in the hay with wife Biddy's cousin, Fidelma? Forget Dick Moran's dirty dealings, Father Devereux's greyhound and Mary eating those magic mushrooms, this was the *Glenroe* storyline that got everyone talking!

RTÉ 2

The unbelievable excitement when Ireland got another TV channel! The new television station launched to great fanfare on 2 November 1978, live from the Cork Opera House. There were messages of support from the great and the good including Michael Parkinson, Bruce Forsyth and Sammy Davis Jr. For many Irish viewers RTÉ 2 was their first chance to see popular UK programmes such as *Top of the Tops* and *Coronation Street*. Or just to enjoy some channel-hopping – from one to the other.

Rule 42

The GAA had always prohibited the playing of non-Gaelic games at their venues. But with plans for the extensive refurbishment of Lansdowne Road Stadium, there were growing calls for them to scrap their Rule 42. After much debate, the GAA finally voted in April 2005 to open Croke Park to other sports. In February 2007, the Irish rugby team took to the pitch to play England in the Six Nations Championship. As 'God Save the Queen' rang out across the stadium that had a century before been the scene of Bloody Sunday, the historic significance was lost on no one.

Ryanair

Remember that time when Michael O'Leary joked that Ryanair was going to start weighing passengers and charging them accordingly? Or that if drink sales are low he gets the pilots to engineer a bit of turbulence? Or what about the time he mentioned putting a coin slot on the toilet door? The Ryanair boss is never short of a controversial comment or two, but the flights are cheap and how else would we get to a random airport on the outskirts of where we actually want to go?

S

Safe Cross Code

Drilled into generations of Irish children, this handy little number reminded us all how to cross the road safely. From finding a safe place to looking all around and listening. And absolutely no leaving the kerb before you've let all the traffic past you. 'Know the Safe Cross Code – KNOW THE CODE.' Somebody tell the jaywalkers!

Saipan

The somewhat unlikely scene of the greatest rift in Irish soccer, between manager Mick McCarthy and star player Roy Keane ahead of the 2002 World Cup finals. Voices were raised, things were said, battle lines were drawn. Even after all these years, the Team Roy or Team Mick question divides families all over the country.

Salad Spinners

In the days before pre-packed rocket and baby leaf spinach, we had to wash our limp lettuce under the tap. Rather than patting it dry with a tea towel, the leafy greens were placed in a sort of tumble dryer for lettuce and given a good spin. Hey presto, your leaves were dry and muck-free, ready for placing on a plate with half a boiled egg, tomato quarters, a slice of rolled-up ham and a good dollop of potato salad.

Sally O'Brien (and the way she might look at you)

This memorable 1980s ad sees an Irish expat, working somewhere very hot and sweaty, thinking wistfully of home and a cold, crisp pint of Harp lager – and getting a beguiling glance from the lovely Sally O'Brien (Vicki Michelle of *'Allo 'Allo!* fame). Rumour had it Taoiseach Charlie Haughey was irked that the actress wasn't even Irish, but thankfully Vicki managed to produce a handy Irish granny.

Saoirse Ronan

One of the youngest actors ever to be nominated for an Oscar, Dubliner Saoirse Ronan was just thirteen when she got the nod for her supporting role in 2007 movie *Atonement.* Now in her late twenties, she has notched up another three nominations – all for Best Actress – for *Brooklyn, Lady Bird* and *Little Women.* Hopefully by the time she wins, the Americans will have finally mastered the pronunciation of her name. It's not rocket science, lads.

Saving Private Ryan

Ireland has played host to lots of Hollywood movies, including *Saving Private Ryan,* which stars Tom Hanks and was directed by Stephen Spielberg here in the summer of 1997. The epic opening scene depicting World War II's D-Day was filmed on Curracloe Beach in Wexford. And half the county will tell you they were an extra in it.

Scrap Saturday

Before *Gift Grub* and *Callan's Kicks*, there was *Scrap Saturday.* This satirical radio show was broadcast on Saturday mornings on RTÉ Radio 1 from 1989 to 1991. Co-written by and starring Dermot Morgan, some of its best-known sketches involved Taoiseach Charles Haughey regaling his long-suffering political advisor, PJ Mara, with his family connections to Julius Caesar, Garibaldi and at least one Doge of Venice. Sounds legit.

Seamus Heaney

Ireland has always punched above its weight when it comes to Nobel Prize laureates for literature. Seamus Heaney, a native of Co. Derry, received the prize in

Stockholm in 1995 'for works of lyrical beauty and ethical depth, which exalt everyday miracles and the living past', making him our fourth recipient after WB Yeats, George Bernard Shaw and Samuel Beckett. Not bad for a little country on the outskirts of Europe.

Self Aid

This one-day event inspired by the success of Live Aid was organised to raise funds for the vast numbers of unemployed people in Ireland. Sixty thousand people made their way to the RDS in 1986 to see the likes of The Boomtown Rats, U2, Bagatelle and The Pogues perform. Broadcast on TV and radio, it was available on modestly priced bootleg VHS and cassettes shortly afterwards.

Shamrock Rovers

In 2011, Shamrock Rovers became the first League of Ireland team ever to reach the Europa League group stages with a 2–1 victory over Partizan Belgrade. They went on to play FC Rubin Kazan, P.A.O.K, and famously take the lead against Spurs at White Hart Lane when Stephen Rice put the ball in the back of the net. The stuff of legend.

Shane Lowry

For the first time in sixty-eight years, The Open, golf's oldest and grandest tournament, came back to Northern Ireland in 2019. Thirty-two-year-old Shane Lowry ensured the Claret Jug would not be leaving the island when he became the fifth Irishman to win the coveted title.

Sheep-Grazing

Over the years, dozens of people have been awarded the Freedom of the City of Dublin including George Bernard Shaw, Gay Byrne and Barack and Michelle Obama. But not all of them have taken its privileges quite as literally as Bono and the Edge who, in 2000, brought lambs to graze in St Stephen's Green. Turns out it was a baa-d idea.

Shirley Temple Bar

One of Ireland's best-known drag queens, Shirley Temple Bar is the alter ego of Declan Buckley and a stalwart of the Irish LGBTQ scene. Renowned for her long-running Sunday-night bingo show in one of Dublin's most famous bars, The George, she became the host of RTÉ's prime time *Telly Bingo* in 2001, with 200,000 viewers tuning in to check their numbers. Eyes down!

Silicon Docks

In 2003, Google set up in Dublin's Docklands with just 100 employees, but that number soon ballooned to 8,000. They have been joined in 'Silicon Docks' by many of the world's biggest tech companies including Facebook, Twitter and Airbnb. Ireland offers a young, well-educated workforce and a handy corporate tax rate, but also damp and temperate weather – greatly reducing energy bills for cooling data systems. Our weather as a plus? Finally! *punches air*

Sinéad O'Connor vs. the Pope

On 3 October 1992, Sinéad O'Connor was the musical guest on US TV show *Saturday Night Live*. In protest at widespread clerical abuse, she held up a photo of Pope John Paul II and ripped it to pieces as she told the audience to 'Fight the real enemy'. There was absolute uproar in the US, and *SNL* made a full apology the following week. Sinéad herself stuck to her guns and remained unrepentant.

Slane

First used for a Thin Lizzy gig in 1981, the grounds of Slane Castle, Co. Meath, regularly played host to the world's biggest musical acts including Dylan, The Stones, Queen, U2, David Bowie, Madonna and Guns N' Roses – and Bruce Springsteen, who played for an epic four hours. With up to 110,000 people attending these gigs in a small and relatively inaccessible village, attendees often have hazy memories of the long midnight walk back to public transport.

Smoking Ban

In 2004, Ireland became – rather unexpectedly for anyone who'd ever lived or socialised here – the first country in the world to outlaw smoking in all enclosed workplaces. Since then, there's mighty craic to be had outside pubs with the huddled smoking masses. And the Irish have become world champion smirters (combined smokers + flirters).

Snow Days

Remember the whoops of kids when, over the years, the country came to a halt as snow covered the country in a thick blanket? Thanks to online learning and Zoom, the next generation of Irish children may never know the unbridled joy of a snow day or a frozen-pipes day. Damn technology!

SodaStream

Everything about SodaStream was iconic: the crème de la crème of '80s drinks and a real treat for the kids. A gas canister was required to give the drinks that special fizz, and the parents wouldn't let just anyone use their machine – that gas doesn't grow on trees, you know! Those curved glass bottles were in short supply too, so children of larger families took a sip of the fizzy deliciousness and passed it on. Grudgingly.

Sonia O'Sullivan

That moment when Sonia O'Sullivan raced over the line at the 2000 Sydney Olympics and took home the silver medal for Ireland in the 5,000m. Back home in Ireland, everyone was glued to their TV screens and willing the Cobh native down the track. A huge win for the nation, and over twenty years later Sonia O'Sullivan is still a household name. Inspiring.

Special Olympics

In June 2003, Ireland hosted the Special Olympics – the first time they had been staged outside the US. It was the biggest sporting event ever to take place here, and boy, did we get involved. Thirty thousand people volunteered to facilitate the athletes, who came from 168 countries worldwide, and U2 and Bon Jovi performed at a special concert in Croke Park. A truly spectacular and joyful event which left its mark on the nation.

The Spire

This pointed, stainless-steel sculpture reaches 120m into the sky from the middle of Dublin's O'Connell Street. Controversial when completed in 2003, as a nation we have grown to love it and allowed it to replace 'under Clery's clock' as the city meeting point. Some of the Spire's more imaginative nicknames include 'The Stiletto in the Ghetto', 'The Nail in the Pale' and 'The Erection at the Intersection'.

Star Wars at Skellig

Eight miles from the coast of Kerry, rising majestically from the sea, are the rocky, uninhabited Skellig islands. A long, long time ago, they were home to one of the earliest monastic settlements in the country and for hundreds of years provided a place of worship for monks. Now the islands are revered by a very different type of pilgrim: *Star Wars* fans. The islands feature prominently in the saga's latest movies. At last, we could legitimately embrace Luke Skywalker as one of our own. We *knew* it.

Stephanie Roche Goal

In 2013, playing for club Peamount United against Wexford Youths, striker Stephanie Roche controlled a cross, flicked the ball over her head and smashed it into the goal from twenty yards out. The stunning goal was captured on camera, and the clip went viral. Roche was nominated for the 2014 FIFA Puskás Award for goal of the year and was the first woman to make it to the final. Goooaaaaal!

Strumpet City

In 1979, O'Connell Street came to a standstill to allow filming of violent scenes depicting clashes between strikers and early twentieth-century Dublin Metropolitan Police. The filming was for the television miniseries based on James Plunkett's epic novel

Strumpet City, portraying the lives of Dubliners in the run-up to the 1913 Lockout and starring Peter O'Toole, Cyril Cusack and David Kelly. At the time it was RTÉ's most successful show, selling to more than thirty countries. Bring it back, we say!

Supermac's

Is there anyone in the country who hasn't ended up in a Supermac's in the wee hours at least once? And for many, it's their favourite go-to chippie. In 2019, the popular Irish fast-food chain won a long-running suit against McDonald's, who had previously put a halt to plans to expand into the UK and Europe because of the similarity between the name Supermac's and their 'Big Mac'. McMadness!

Sweet Cigarettes

White, chalky sticks of sugar with a little glow of red colouring at one end, packaged up like real cigarettes and marketed with Superman branding. A generation of kids faux-puffing away on them. What could possibly go wrong??

'The Sweetest Thing'

Do you remember that time Bono didn't make it home in time to celebrate his wife Ali's birthday so he wrote her a song, and then got Boyzone to appear in the video? That's the kind of thing you can do when you're Bono.

T

Takeaway Pints

For a nation that loves its pints, it took a pandemic for us to realise that, just like coffee, beer could be taken away and savoured sitting on a wall or green. This is one pandemic trend that might be here to stay.

Tayto Park

An amusement park based on a crisp? Yes, that's right. In November 2010, Tayto Park opened up on the outskirts of Ashbourne in Co. Meath. Home to Europe's largest wooden rollercoaster, the Cú Chulainn Coaster, it also has a zoo, a crisp factory and free Tayto crisps when you leave. Nice!

Ten Pence Bars

These teeth-breaking, E number-filled delights were hugely popular in 1980s Ireland. Take your pick from Big Time, Macaroon, Mint Crisp, Klipso, Roy of the Rovers, Dennis the Menace, Stinger or Wham. Fillings not included.

TG4

Ireland's Irish-language station, located in the west of

Ireland, launched in 1996. As well as producing *Ros na Rún*, Ireland's first soap opera as Gaeilge, the rural TV channel was responsible for launching the careers of Dáithí Ó Sé and sisters Gráinne and Síle Seoige. Go raibh maith agaibh from a grateful nation.

'Thank You Very Much, Mr Eastwood'

A novelty single from comedy genius Dermot Morgan that made the Christmas No 1 spot in 1985. It played on boxing world champion Barry McGuigan's repeated thanking of his manager, Barney Eastwood, and featured Morgan's impressions of not only McGuigan but the holy '80s trinity of the Pope, Ronald Reagan and Bob Geldof.

Thunder and Lightning

On the night of 25 July 1985, Ireland was hit by one of the worst lightning storms it had ever seen. The hailstones were so big they damaged crops, and hundreds of animals died from being struck by lightning. Children from all over the country watched in awe from their bedroom windows as forks of lightning charged through the night sky. Unnecessary journeys were definitely discouraged.

Tightening our Belts

Ireland was faced with the biggest trade deficit in the history of the state when Taoiseach Charlie Haughey took to the national broadcaster before the 1980 budget to advise the general public that 'we are living away beyond our means'. This from the man who was later found out to have spent £15,800 on Parisian shirts.

The Tommy Tiernan Show

It is the most bizarre of concepts: Tommy Tiernan interviews guests from the world of entertainment, sport and current affairs, but until they sit down in front of him, the comedian has no idea who they are. This means zero time to research or prepare questions, which has made for some great off-the-cuff moments with guests like Sharon Horgan, Imelda May and Eddie Izzard. With ratings topping even those of *The Late Late Show*, the unpredictability has proved a big hit.

Tony McCoy

In November 2013, Tony McCoy became the first jump jockey to ride 4,000 winners when he took the top spot at Towcester with the JP McManus-owned Mountain

Tunes. He retired in 2015, having been champion jockey every season since his first as a professional. Impressive!

Tour de France

In the summer of 1987, when Stephen Roche and Sean Kelly were at the height of their cycling careers, Dubliner Roche battled his way through twenty-five tough stages to clinch victory at the Tour de France. That summer every Irish kid was out on their bike, pedalling their little legs as fast as they could and dreaming of wearing the yellow jersey one day. All the free Galtee cheese would just be the icing on the cake.

Toy Show Tickets

Back in 2008, the nation gasped when poor Barbara, a competition winner from Cork, had the nerve to tell Pat Kenny she wanted the ten grand prize but wasn't interested in the much sought after *Toy Show* tickets. Pat was very put out and promptly ripped up the pair of tickets live on air, leaving viewers gaping at their TV screens in shock. Barbara, how could you?

Trinity College

In 1970, the Church finally lifted its hundred-year-old
ban on Catholics attending Trinity College. The ban
had been imposed on the grounds that attendance at the
prestigious university, which was founded under Queen
Elizabeth I, constituted 'a moral danger to the faith of
Irish Catholics'. In fairness, Rag Week is a moral danger
to many a first year.

Twister

Like most of Ireland, Donegal has its share of changeable
weather – but there's changeable and then there's
tornadoes! In 2012, a 700-metre-high twister more
synonymous with the US hit Slieve Sneacht near
Buncrana, Co. Donegal. You never know, perhaps there
will be a Las Vegas in the hills of Donegal some day!

U

U2 at Croke Park

It seems apt that the first band to perform a headline gig at Croke Park were U2, on 29 June 1985. Fans shelled out £12.50 for a golden ticket to see the Dublin boys live, fresh from a sold-out Madison Square Garden gig and backed up by a young REM, no less. They travelled from far and wide, often in smoke-filled Bus Éireann buses crammed with naggin-swilling young folk, many of them destined for Hill 16, which – rumour had it – was the place for the more ardent couples. One over-enthusiastic fan who managed to climb up onto the roof of the Cusack Stand was gently admonished and asked to descend to safety by Bono with the wise words, 'It's alright to have a hard neck but not a broken neck.' Possibly the pinnacle of that young lad's life.

Under the Hawthorn Tree

First published in 1990, this moving novel by Marita Conlon-McKenna tells the story of three young children and their struggle for survival during one of the darkest periods in Ireland's history, the Famine. Still as popular as ever, it has become a modern classic. Is there a child in the country who didn't have it read to them by their primary school teacher?

'Unnecessary Journeys'

In 2015, Storm Desmond battered the west coast of Ireland, causing severe flood damage. But that's not what it will be remembered for; it will forever be the storm that made Teresa Mannion a household name. The RTÉ TV presenter was broadcasting from Galway city when she uttered the immortal words: 'Don't make unnecessary journeys. Don't take risks on treacherous roads.' The clip racked up millions of views and a viral star was born.

US Presidential Visits

Lots of sitting US presidents have caused a sensation by popping over to check out their Irish homesteads, including JFK, Ronald Reagan, Bill Clinton and Barack O'Bama. In all, we Irish unashamedly claim no fewer than twenty US presidents as our own, from Andrew Jackson to Abraham Lincoln to Bushes senior and junior. Sure, where would they be without us? (Disclaimer: we accept no responsibility whatever for Trump. Definitely not one of ours.)

V

Vaccine

Who knew we would all become vaccine aficionados?!
But we have. We know our AstraZeneca from our Pfizer
and our Moderna from our Johnson & Johnson. 'Which
one did you get?' is the new conversation starter!

'Very Particular Set of Skills'

Nobody predicted that Oscar nominee and national
institution Liam Neeson would become Hollywood's
favourite action star at the age of fifty-six, but what an
unexpected gift to the genre. In 2008's *Taken*, he plays
an ex-CIA man whose daughter has been kidnapped
in Paris. Neeson tells her captors – via his surprisingly
low-tech phone – about his 'very particular set of skills'
that will help him find and kill them. Possibly the most
mangled film quote of all time.

Vicar Street

The home of Irish comedy since 1998, Vicar Street has
played host to a string of comedians from Dylan Moran
to Dara Ó Briain and Maeve Higgins to Des Bishop.
But it's Tommy Tiernan who holds the record for the
longest-running performance at the Dublin venue, with

166 performances of his *Loose* show in 2004–2005. Now that's a long run.

Viennetta

There was a time in Ireland when you couldn't get posher than Viennetta. It was the epitome of class and saved for Sundays after the roast. Creamy ice cream with chocolate ripples throughout that cracked satisfyingly when you took a delicious bite. Yum!

Virgin Megastore

The curious case of the Virgin condoms. In 1989, Richard Branson flew into Ireland to testify in court on behalf of the Irish Family Planning Association. Their crime: operating a stall selling condoms at his flagship Virgin Megastore on Aston Quay, when it was illegal to sell them outside a pharmacy. The IFPA were fined £400 and multimillionaire Richard Branson happily forked out the cash for them.

Volcano!

Remember that time in 2010 when people's holiday plans had to be cancelled? Not because of a worldwide pandemic, but due to volcanic ash from the eruption of Eyjafjallajökull in Iceland. The ash formed clouds above Europe's airspace and disrupted air traffic across northern and western Europe for eight days. When the coronavirus arrived, we would look back on Eyjafjallajökull as the good old days ...

W

'Wagon Wheel'

In 2012, a young country singer from Liverpool took the Irish country music scene by storm with a cover of this song. It went mainstream and made Nathan Carter a household name. The song was written by none other than Bob Dylan. Yes, that Bob Dylan. And what a touching tribute to childhood biscuits it is.

Wanderly Wagon

Airing on RTÉ from 1967 to 1982, this was a much-loved TV show about a flying covered wagon and a motley crew of human and puppet characters including O'Brien and Godmother, Judge the dog, the bearded sweetshop owner Fortycoats (who even got his own spin-off), and arch-villain Sneaky Snake, voiced by Frank Kelly. Mention it to Irish forty- and fifty-somethings and watch them get all teary-eyed with nostalgia.

Westlife Farewell Tour

After fourteen years together, Westlife announced they would be playing their final gig ever in Dublin's Croke Park as part of their 2012 farewell tour. The band performed in front of a crowd of 80,000 fans, many of whom were inconsolable. But fast-forward a few years: the boys realised how much they missed performing together and – hey presto – they were back. More of a 'See ya later' than a farewell, really.

'What's Another Year?'

Johnny Logan won the Eurovision Song Contest with this cracker in 1980. The contest was held in The Hague, the Netherlands, and was Ireland's second victory of the much-loved competition. The song went on to reach number one in seven countries and started the nation's love affair with Johnny and his white suit.

Where in the World?

This Sunday-night game show hosted by Marty Whelan, and then Theresa Lowe, pitted two families against each other in a bid to win the top prize of a family holiday. Broadcast from 1987 to 1996, it was the warm-up act for everyone's favourite Irish drama, *Glenroe*, and at its height had over one million viewers. Geography was never more fun.

Where's Grandad?

This was just one of a series of harrowing water-safety ads that appeared on Irish television throughout the 1980s. The ads are so shocking that it is hard to believe they were actually aired. Look them up on YouTube at your peril. And do not leave your grandad sitting in a deckchair at the edge of a lake!

'Where's Me Jumper?'

A bona fide Cork classic, this anarchic tune from the Sultans of Ping FC was released in February 1992 and went to No 8 in the Irish music charts. It has stood the test of time though, and appears on every list of the best-ever Irish songs. The lyrics vividly capture every young fella's worse nightmare: lost knitwear.

'Whiskey in the Jar'

Despite not particularly liking the song themselves, 'Whiskey in the Jar' proved to be the song that launched Thin Lizzy internationally. In 1973, the song went to No 6 in the UK charts and secured twenty-three-year-old Phil Lynott and his band a coveted spot on *Top of the Pops*. They later dropped the song from their live sets but at that stage had plenty of hits to keep any audience well entertained.

White Ladder

David Gray released the album *White Ladder* in 1998 and with the help of Donal Dineen's RTÉ show, *No Disco*, the music-loving Irish fell hard for the Manchester-born, Welsh-raised singer-songwriter. *White Ladder* ended up being the country's best-selling album of all time – it's rumoured there isn't a house in Ireland that doesn't have a copy.

'Who's in the House?'

The novelty rap by Fr Brian and the Fun Lovin' Cardinals, AKA the journalist and presenter Brendan O'Connor, was released in 2000 and hit No 3 in the Irish charts. It parodied attempts by the Catholic Church to be cool and 'down with the kids'. Jesus in the House. That's who.

The Wicklow Way

Ireland's first designated waymarked, long-distance walking trail was opened in 1980. The 127km-long trail begins in Rathfarnham, travelling across Wicklow and finishing in the town of Clonegal, Co. Carlow. Wicklow is known as the garden county, and a hike along the route reveals exactly why. If you would like to complete the entire trail, give yourself five to seven days and don't forget the snacks!

Wild Mountain Thyme

It may have been fortunate that cinemas were closed when this doozie hit the big screen in 2020. *Wild Mountain Thyme* has every cliché going, even the dreaded pan pipes playing in the background. And despite actually being Irish, Jamie Dornan's brogue was criticised as being up there with Tom Cruise's in *Far and Away*. Poor Emily Blunt's character can't pronounce a 'th' to save her life. But begorrah, she does love dese rolling green fields and all dat type of ting.

Willie O'Dea

As part of a demonstration by the elite Army Ranger Wing in 2005, Minister for Defence Willie O'Dea posed with a gun pointing straight at the camera. The photograph was published in three national newspapers, including the front page of *The Irish Times*. Minister for Defence with a gun pointing out from the pages of a newspaper ... sometimes there is such a thing as bad publicity.

The Wind That Shakes the Barley

In 2006, Ken Loach's thought-provoking film about the Irish War of Independence and Civil War scooped the prestigious Palme d'Or at the Cannes Film Festival. A pre-*Peaky Blinders* Cillian Murphy starred as one of two Cork brothers who fight together for independence but find themselves on opposite sides after the treaty is signed. Bring tissues.

Wood Quay

In 1978, twenty thousand people took to the streets in protest at the proposed bulldozing of Wood Quay, a prime archaeological site for Dublin's Viking and Norman heritage, to make way for Dublin Corporation's new headquarters. A number of protestors went on to occupy the site the following year. If events at Wood Quay happened today, there is little doubt that it would have been handled differently. But despite the strong public backlash, the works continued and much of the city's heritage was lost to make way for a bastion of 1970s architecture, making history of history.

A Woman's Heart

Ask someone what song they were humming back
in 1992 and odds-on it was the sorrowful title track
by Eleanor McEvoy from the mega-popular album
A Woman's Heart. McEvoy joined Mary Black,
Dolores Keane, Frances Black, Maura O'Connell and
accordionist extraordinaire Sharon Shannon in songs
about life and loss, tears and trouble: oh, their hearts
were low, their hearts were so low. But selling a record-
breaking one million copies worldwide must have eased
the pain, just a little.

X

The X Factor

In 2010, a Mullingar teenager took to the stage in Croke Park and performed in front of the *X Factor* judges for the first time. The judges liked his personality more than his performance but put him through to the next stage nonetheless. The rest, as they say, is history, and Niall Horan went on to become one-fifth of One Direction, the world's most successful boy band ever. Not too bad for a sixteen-year-old 'from the midlands of Ireland'.

X-rated

Tagged as a 'Novel You Will Never Forget', Alan Shatter's *Laura* was published in 1989, the story of a young Oireachtas secretary who falls in love with a dashing TD and then gives up their love child for adoption. It caused a storm years after first publication when someone dug up the sex scene and splashed it around, so to speak. There are some things you just don't want to imagine your Minister for Justice writing. *shudder*

Y

Yes

On Saturday, 23 May 2015, Ireland made history by becoming the first country in the world to legalise same-sex marriage by popular vote. Voters had gone to the polls the day before with the results being announced at a crowded event in the courtyard at Dublin Castle. Early indications pointed towards a majority yes vote and, in the end, a whopping 62% of the Irish Republic's electorate chose to let people marry whoever they love. YES!

'Young People of Ireland'

In 1979, when Pope John Paul II became the first pope to visit Ireland, over a million ardent Catholics attended his mass in the Phoenix Park. But it was at a 300,000-strong youth mass at Ballybrit Racecourse that he uttered the most memorable words of his visit: 'Young people of Ireland, I love you.' Almost forty years later, Pope Francis became the second Pontiff to set foot on Irish soil. But Ireland was a changed country, and the only reason young people would be heading to Ballybrit was for the Galway Races.

'You Wouldn't Be Long Getting Frostbit'

Eighteen-year-old Ruairi McSorley became an overnight sensation when he was interviewed on UTV news about the snowfall around his home in the Sperrin Mountains. His Northern Irish accent and old-fashioned turn of phrase had viewers turning to YouTube in their millions to replay those immortal words. Subtitles *on*.

Z

Zig and Zag Return

The hilarious characters from RTÉ 2's *The Den* kept '80s
and '90s kids entertained weekdays after school with their
madcap antics and alter egos Captain Joke, Cousin Nigel
and Sunny Daze, and additional characters Zuppy, Dustin
the Turkey, Soky and the evil Podge. To everyone's delight
the boys reunited with presenter Ray D'Arcy in 2020 to
lift the nation's spirits. Yay!

'Zombie'

A protest song penned by the late Cranberries lead
singer Dolores O'Riordan that went on to become a huge
worldwide hit. A multitude of cover versions have been
uploaded online in lots of genres including death metal,
punk, choral, classical, soul and jazz. In 2020 the song
became the first by an Irish band to reach one billion
plays on YouTube. Iconic.

Zoo

When Ireland entered a second lockdown in 2020 during
the worldwide pandemic, Dublin Zoo pleaded for the
country's help. Without visitors, the Zoo warned, it might
have to close its doors permanently. The nation rallied and

within twelve hours over a million euro was raised. We love you, Dublin Zoo!

ABOUT THE AUTHORS

Both children of the 1980s, Kunak and Sarah were big fans of the Safe Cross Code, Fat Frogs and roller skates. They still cry when they watch the 'Nothing Compares 2 U' video and are known to swoon slightly when they see Johnny Logan in a white suit. They're only human. Their previous books include *The A to Z of Being Irish*, *Irish Mammy in Your Pocket* and *The A to Z of an Irish Christmas*.

Also by Sarah Cassidy & Kunak McGann:

Ever wondered about the healing powers of dock leaves, flat 7UP and Sudocrem? Confused about the difference between 'going out' and 'going out-out'? This handy A to Z is packed with insider knowledge and quirky Irishisms for locals and blow-ins alike.

We can't be doing with Calling Birds, French Hens or Partridges in Pear Trees, but if it's Annuals, The Dinner, The Big Shop or The Wexford Carol you're looking for, you've come to the right book!

From the weather to your choice of clothing, the quintessential Irish Mam has something to say on every subject. This handy collection of Mammyisms will ensure you are never without her words of wisdom.